PRAISE
BE STILL AND KN

"This book is a clear inquiry into the true nature of Who You Really Are. An intelligent presentation of a dialogue with your own Heart and a great addition to your non-dual library. Highly recommended!"

Chuck Hillig

Author of *Enlightenment for Beginners*, *The Way IT Is*, and *Looking for God: Seeing the Whole in One*

"This wise, skillful book presents profound insights that resonate with the non-dual (Advaita) teachings of Ramana Maharshi, Eckhart Tolle, Krishnamurti, and Nisargadatta Maharaj. In succinct dialogues between the archetypal human and the Divine Reality, the reader is confronted with the layers of egoic illusion that cloud perception of what is Real. The Voice heard in this volume is firm, direct, loving, compassionate, and familiar with the suffering of all those who believe themselves to be separate individuals alienated from the Ground of Being. This book is strong medicine and will surely find its way to those searching for authentic awakening."

Phillip Lucas, Ph.D.

Professor of Religious Studies, Stetson University

"This is a gem of a book ... Through it all, the God who dialogues with this human self is himself human in personality, by turns forgiving, challenging, humorous, truculent, and in every sense wise."

Nowick Gray
Editor of *Alternative Culture Magazine*

"*Be Still and Know I AM God* belongs in every 'spiritual tool kit' for developing 'conscious contact with a Higher Power.' It is truly one of the 'helpful books' and its message was very important for me. I highly recommend it to all who are working such a program."

Dave Fine
Publisher of *The Solution News*

Nick Gancitano lives with his wife Penelope and together they have formed The Self-Inquiry Center, an organization whose purpose and function is to share the Self-Inquiry. In his writings and seminars, he assists those who desire to realize who they are.

Emergent from his background in American football, business and education, Nick drew from his personal experiences of yoga and meditation to direct athletes in their performance, before teaching these principles to the general public. Nick frequently tours the world, responding to requests for lectures and offering workshops to support and spread the messages contained in the book *Be Still and Know I AM God*.

To contact Nick visit: www.www.nickgancitano.com

BE STILL AND KNOW I AM GOD

The Direct Path to
Knowing God Within

NICK GANCITANO

Cygnus

CYGNUS PUBLICATIONS

This edition first published in the UK in 2012 by
Cygnus Publications, Innovation Centre, Bristol & Bath Science Park,
Dirac Crescent, Emersons Green, Bristol BS16 7FR

1 3 5 7 9 10 8 6 4 2

Designed and typeset by Jerry Goldie Graphic Design

Printed and bound by CPI UK

British Library Cataloguing-in-Publication Data Available
Library of Congress Cataloging-in-Publication Data Available

ISBN: 978-0-95493-267-1

www.cygnus-books.co.uk

The intention of this book
is to awaken you to the Truth
I AM

The little saying, "Be still and know that I Am God" ... contains the entire wisdom of religion in those few words.

Eckhart Tolle

CONTENTS

ACKNOWLEDGMENTS

I would like to thank Hippocampus-BRT Ltd., creators of the Lenyo LUX™ Electromagnetic Bio-Communication Device, whose equipment neutralized incoherent ELF/VLF computer emissions, making it possible for this book to be created on the computer. (www.hippocampus-brt.com)

INTRODUCTION

You who have searched for spiritual sustenance, having turned away time and time again from some religion, guru or *Master* and are as yet still unfulfilled, the reason being that most paths to awakening have been corrupted through the mistranslation of scriptures that neglect to address contemporary concerns in such a way that neutralizes the unconsciousness of the world today:

Be not dismayed, for in your hands now rests the *most direct path* to Knowing God within, that which all religions and philosophies attempt to convey, yet have failed to articulate as a complete work. In response, *Be Still and Know I AM God* embodies all elements necessary for you to awaken to the Truth. This Message is so essential that its content will allow your consciousness to fully recognize I AM within and have been all along, guiding and providing for you in all you do. Who am I? I AM Your True Self, the One and only God. Once knowing that I AM within, you will release your attachment to the body and this world, allowing you to fulfill your destiny. In order to do this without attracting resistance, the ego must be shed so you may be a pillar of integrity, abandoning your conditioning and destructive mind patterns that have thus far prevented you from turning within, so I can restore you to My Heavenly Kingdom.

Return to this book as necessary, halting the impulse to read endless books. As you read, I urge you to consider each sentence *carefully* before proceeding on to the next, pausing to permit the deeper meaning within each passage to open your heart so your mind can awaken to the light, erasing the residue that has prevented you from remembering the Truth. If you are empty of preconceptions and your mind is still, you will resonate with what I AM presenting to you and recognize *That* which you have been yearning for.

I will neither flood your mind with useless facts nor persuade you to forsake your own experience, for most of what you have learned thus far was forged from the beliefs of *others*. Instead, I ask you here to ignore all you have learned since that knowledge was necessary only so you would succumb to the world illusion, yet it is now counterproductive for you to continue holding on to those beliefs, nor should you turn the contents of what is here into another religion if it is your intention to awaken.

You will be astonished by the content herein that symbolizes your life, for it is likely you spent your early life attempting to satisfy others and receive their approval, only later discovering the futility of those efforts, when you realized that truth must come from your own direct experience and not borrowed religious beliefs, formal education, the media or societal conditioning, all of which fail to lead humanity from its dismal mass hypnosis, the mind-numbing effect of ubiquitous stimuli that bombard you morning until night, seducing you to consume more and become someone you are not in order to sustain a bleak picture of reality as humanity suffers under the crippling effects of incoherent technology systems, the barren global economy and a political agenda that has repeatedly demonstrated its inability to empower the people or provide them with basic needs and vital information necessary to do so themselves.

At first glance, *Be Still and Know I AM God* may appear to be one man's personal communication with God, yet as you read on you will recognize your Self in both voices, for both are Yours, confronting ignorance in the light of Truth. Hence, I encourage you to read as though I AM addressing you directly. To comprehend this, you must first recognize that you have been pretending to be a separate individual with a *personal story*, like a finite point in Infinite space, while in Reality You Are that Infinite space itself. If this sounds peculiar, continue on and I will engage your higher wisdom, revealing to you the significance of what I AM now presenting you.

The ideas contained here are designed to have you challenge your conditioning, including your undisputed laws of society, religious dogmas, cherished human ideals and even your concept of reality itself. Perhaps you have wondered *What is Reality*? If this question intrigues you, then what I reveal here will arouse you, for the misinformation you have accumulated thus far has kept you in bondage. Indeed, what you have learned in the traditional sense is not even true or *Real*, for what you have been calling *reality* is actually a mirage of solidity.

So *Be Present* as I reiterate specific points and chisel away at the dense layers of ego, dismantling those cornerstones that have supported its structure, which up to this point has prevented you from Knowing the Truth of Who You Really Are. Read as in prayer or meditation and allow this *Process* to dissolve any confusion so You Will Know That You Are God. To understand this, allow these words to penetrate your consciousness, for this Message is the seed of Truth You have planted for the moment You desire to awaken to the dream – and that moment is Now.

CHAPTER ONE

I AM

Who is this, God?

Yes.

So this is how it happens?

Not always.

Well, I'm confused and I don't know who I am.

Are you sure about that?

No, but I think I know who You are.

There are no divisions – we are One and the same.

So why bother with this world at all?

It is no bother for Me. Is it bothersome for you?

Totally. I'm utterly confused about life.

Good.

Why good?

Because you are realizing you don't know anything.

Yeah. It's all ... I don't know – pointless.

What is?

Me, going around in circles, the same thing day after day.

It is what it is. Nothing more.

But I don't know what the fuck's happening, and here I am talking to myself. Are You really God?

It's All God, so it is best if you stop splitting It up.

What exactly do You mean by "God"?

God is the I AM consciousness, the Impersonal state of awareness; It is knowing that "I Exist." In fact, you could not even have this communication or read this if you did not exist, because you must first Be in order to be conscious of any-*thing*. In other words, the light of your awareness, God, *must always be turned on or nothing could appear to you.*

All is composed of the one I AM substance, the all-pervasive, invisible substratum that underlies all life and form everywhere, just as a movie screen is within a motion picture: the screen never changes, even when the picture-images do. Yet in Reality the screen is Self-aware; and all the while I AM observes its creation through you.

Why do I not recognize this I AM?

Is the actor's image on the movie screen aware of the screen? Also, That which is always here can be difficult to recognize. If It never comes or leaves, how could you notice It? How could you Be aware of some-*thing* unless there is some One within, aware of that thing? I AM that One within – I AM the sense of Eternal Awareness, That which always Is. I AM That, which is unchanging and aware even as your body, thoughts and life circumstances change.

Why is it so difficult to recognize that I am one with You?

A fish can only recognize it was in the ocean once it is removed, yet you cannot be removed from the ocean of consciousness by which you could reflect upon It and say "Look, there is consciousness over there and now I am here, separate from It." As such, you are equipped with the internal capacity to realize You are consciousness, so there is no need to remove your *self* from It, nor could you do so. There is no boundary that you can cross and glance back to say, "There It is." Yet, by deepening your awareness of Self, you feel a melting of imaginary boundaries where form meets formlessness and You become aware that You are One with All.

How can I be certain I'm communicating with God here?

Does this feel like Love or resonate as Truth?

Yes. Yet how can I be sure?

When your mind is still, your heart opens and the indescribable fills you.

So if it doesn't feel like Love, then it's not God?

Not what you would call the highest expression of God; I AM appearing to you in every conceivable way; even now I AM being perceived as a mere thought.

So You really are God?

As you would have Me Be.

Where are You?

Here.

Where is here?

Everywhere. I AM what Is.

How can I know that?

What do you think it would be like to be inside the sun?

I don't know, I guess it would be awfully bright, and so hot that I couldn't even be solid.

Do you realize that you are in the sun right now? That the sun extends out beyond anything you are physically aware of? The only reason you did not recognize this is because you were told differently. You were taught you are separate from it; the sun is "up there" and you are "down here." Yet even though you can feel the heat of the sun, you still denied your feelings for what you were told. So then, what would it be like to be inside God, as God? Just as with the sun, you were taught that God is up there and you are down here. The reason most cannot recognize the obvious is because they have ignored their inner awareness and become desensitized. Yet one must be even more sensitive to perceive consciousness than to feel physical heat since unconditioned consciousness is not determinate. So when one is incapable of deep sensitivity, one will resort to believing what others teach over their own experience.

That's so obvious. So now what?

Everything and nothing is happening.

What?

You said, "I don't know what the fucks happening."

Please don't do that.

What is *that* exactly?

Curse.

Confront your fear of words. You must face all that you are afraid of.

I'm not afraid, it just bothers me when God curses.

It threatens your concept of God.

Something like that.

Then it is good, because your concept of God must completely die, or I AM unable to appear to you as I truly AM. You have objectified consciousness, which is not an object, and then proceeded to pin your religious dogmas on that "object." Yet I AM formless, so on "what" can you attach your fictions?

I thought You could Be whatever You desire.

I have no desire, I AM Infinite. It is the soul that strives to become more, thus it projects limitations onto Me.

Why is desiring to become more a limitation?

Desiring to *become* more unconsciously affirms that one is not enough. And when one affirms, one makes It *firm*, manifesting that one is *that idea*. This is how unconscious creation works: one always affirms what one gives attention to. So each thought or resistance to a thought, if persisted in, makes that thought real.

How can resisting a thought make it real?

Do you resist something if you think it is not real?

No, I guess not.

What you think about grows and solidifies into fact. Also, when you resist something, it condenses in consciousness, where the universe originates.

All ideas come *to* you, not *from* you. That is, the *you* that you believe you are. And once thoughts enter the brain, the intellect assesses and judges each thought as good or bad, pleasurable or painful. If they are considered pleasurable, they recycle, energizing creation with that feeling; if painful, the intellect retains that thought within one's imagination to evaluate or resist the thought. The intellect's image is then reinforced with sensory input and divides its perception of the experiences, converting them into isolated mishaps – when all that happens is really My Will and perfectly interconnected.

When will I have the clarity to know Your voice is mine?

Now. You must choose this for your *self*.

I have felt the urge to grow beyond my idea of You as a personal God.

Yes, it is best to look to the I AM inside and not as an external form. Although you should realize this communication could not even occur to you if you were not aware of Me within already.

Will I be confused if I eliminate this dependency on You?

Confusion is a natural part of the awakening process while one transcends the religious concept of a personal God to discover the True Impersonal God within.

So, You're saying that God is not personal?

I AM saying that I AM not a person.

I still feel like I need You for support.

Where could I possibly go? I AM always here.

But how can I stand alone if I cut the umbilical cord?

There is no cord, we are One.

So You will help me Know I AM God?

Yes, as I have been preparing you all along.

What will be different?

You will be more reliant on intuition, instinct and feeling, and less dependent on the intellect. It will all come back to you because the Truth is Your Nature. If uncertain, you may always meditate on the significance of this passage:

Be Still, and Know, I AM, God

I feel that.

Yes, because it is True.

Now earlier You said the intellect is limited. Why?

The intellect is used to interpret relationships and create divisions, so it projects errors, analyzes, and establishes boundaries where none actually exist. That is its function as the primary limiting aspect of consciousness, so all fears and illusion arise from its biased inferences.

There must be a reason for the intellect though.

Yes. The intellect splits the mind, which allows analysis, categorizing and judgment. It serves as a tool when I AM expressing a limited aspect of Being, yet it is unnecessary when I AM awakening from the illusion.

When my intellect is active, how can I bring it into stillness?

Do not try so hard and be intent on knowing I AM. Have faith so you can feel I AM within and receive.

What about giving?

Live to give and you will know the glory of Being God.

If I were unhappy, how could I give or interact with people and not be a burden to them?

Become aware of the unhappiness then let it pass, yet do not resist it or complain. You need not smile when you are around people, just remain aware that I AM and you have turned your burdens over to Me. By simply Being aware of *awareness*, there is never a need to be unhappy.

When you Know You Are God, you must give, not

because you are obligated, but because you cannot contain your joy, which radiates outward to and through All. This is Presence and one can offer nothing more valuable than Presence. Only that of the flesh requires you to give in a way perceivable to the physical eye, yet when you know You Are the formless "I," then you are giving Your Self to All.

Is it good to give to the homeless or stray animals?

As you wish, and so long as you do not feel obligated or superior to them while doing so. Only then will the giving not be motivated by ego and self-righteousness. Know that anytime you feel sorry for someone else, this is the ego tempting you to pity another, which disempowers them and reinforces that degrading idea, cementing that *reality* in consciousness. Pity is arrogance disguised as compassion, yet true compassion is not pity at all, but holding the highest ideal for all, which is seeing all as Your Self.

This ideal is seeing all as content and happy whether they acknowledge it or not. This way, you do not project your concepts or pictures of reality onto other forms, but instead hold a clear and loving image of them that serves their highest vision.

I noticed that You don't treat me as inferior even when I sin.

What is this "you" and "I"? I do not treat you as though you are inferior, because I AM You. And why should I care if you're angry or if you curse? So long as you are passionate, a "curse" word can be a genuine manner by which to convey a message without repressing. How delightful it is to be unrestrained by the conforms of society and not resist your emotions.

So You're good with it?

I AM good with It all – I Love It All.

That helps me not feel guilty anymore.

The true sin, as you put it, would be to not express when the impulse arises, which would repress the emotion and generate disease. I AM not saying to make curse words a majority of your vocabulary, yet if one should emerge then don't hold back, recognizing it is I who AM doing it anyway. Also, be aware of whether it is aimed at others with intent to do harm. If this is the case, conscious restraint may be in order so as to not escalate a situation.

CHAPTER TWO

RELIGION

Why do I see so many people leaving organized religion?

Religions are training wheels for spiritual seekers, so they are falling off because people's intelligence has evolved beyond the need for them. They are realizing the Truth without the dependency on outside organizations that preach borrowed beliefs rather than encourage one to trust one's own experience when Truth can never be discovered in the former way.

What is all the repression about?

When feelings of guilt and being judged become too painful they are repressed, and the fear of being exposed manifests as rage, which when further repressed becomes depression. This is how depression has recently become pandemic in the world, because most religions have persuaded people that anger is wrong. This suppression has become a disease, and the prescribing of anti-depressants is likewise ignorant and founded in greed.

How is this related to religion?

Religious morality promotes shame and therefore repression, which consequently becomes depression. Preaching morality is unconscious arrogance. This arrogance implies I cannot express *directly* through those who are looking for direction. So, one need not use drugs or attempt to guide others; offer your loving presence instead.

If people felt they were being guided by You, maybe they wouldn't need to look for guidance elsewhere.

This is the ego's standard response, yet realize that one only turns to another for advice when one *refuses to surrender*. For if one surrenders, where is the need for guidance once it is realized there is no other?

It is best to forget about organized religions and the scriptures of the past. What I prescribe for you now is on a private basis. True-life spirituality is living life, not congregating like cattle to listen to pontification. So release yourself: play, dance, sing, make love, experience nature, laugh, cry, or even go for naked walks in the park with your dog.

Whatsoever, be creative and enthusiastic in all aspects of life. Live passionately – without holding back. Allow for emotional eruptions and sensual expression. Then feel the contrast of a new world untainted by fear or restrictions. Stop learning about morality from your preachers and go experience life.

But I've been to some fun churches.

I AM not *only* talking about having fun. I AM talking

about Truth, Love and Freedom. If one thinks they need to go somewhere to receive My Message, they have been misled to depend on outside sources, when I AM always here within. Be wary of parroting a preacher's words upon demand, for each word is creative, and if you are not conscious of their context or meaning these unconscious utterances can attract rather undesirable consequences.

Would You give me an example?

Wedding vows. One who desires freedom does not get entangled in commitments beyond the Now. You can ask directly what you will of Me; you require no middleman. Hence, why come to Me through someone else when you can turn directly within?

Maybe people are intimidated by You?

Yes, religions have made it so. How can someone surrender if they are frightened? And why are you afraid? Because what is being shared in religions is not love at all, but behavior control. Many even attend temples of worship to *appear* righteous, believing that I do not know the difference.

Why do You require my surrender if You're egoless?

Who are you surrendering to but your Self? I AM You and You are All That Is. I AM that inner Presence within, felt as "I." By loving Me, you love All That Is, including everyone and everything. Many have even been taught by religions to fear Me, yet I AM the mirror of one's own

Image and Likeness, so what one sees in one's self, one will also see in Me. By loving All of one's Self, surrender happens naturally.

Should one bypass God and go directly to this "I"?

They are the same, so whatever suits one is best.

The Bible says You are vengeful. Is this true?

Yes, I AM, yet you should understand the meaning of the word if you are to use it. To be vengeful is to respond with equal measure; it is the law of karma. When you hit something, do you not hurt your hand? So you learn not to hit. The hard surface is teaching you: Will you listen to its message or continue to inflict suffering upon your *self*? It is compassionate to respond, so you learn to love and not be aggressive. Would you expect anything different? How can you learn if I do not reflect behavior? How will you experience Your Self if I AM not a mirror for You? I have said "Do unto others as you would have them do unto you." Why? Because they are You. One attacks others only when one expects attack from others, even if the other is really one's Self.

What about participation in ritual or ceremony?

If you are sincere in knowing your Self, you must move beyond religion altogether and allow Me to direct you in all ways. Rituals can be a tricky *business* so, it is best to turn inward and forego these external sentiments, for if you ask, I will guide you directly.

But are there any benefits to ritual and ceremony?

The intention behind all action is what determines its effectiveness and utility. In any case, one may inquire: To whom would these benefits occur? The answer is "To me." Then inquire "Who am I?" Knowing that You are formless awareness, no such superficial gestures are required, for ceremonies are a process of setting forth context, which functions as a limiting structure. The greatest of contexts is I AM, which encompasses All, thus eliminating the need for any ritual, ceremony or other sentiments. Ask, "What is my intention in Life?" For if your intention is to realize the Truth, then you need not engage in religious ceremony and rituals, which only sustain a false notion of personal volition. The most direct path to the Truth is to Know I AM, which bypasses religions, traditions and all superficial ideologies. As such, ceremonies are for those who would rather pretend they are going within than actually go there.

Once I felt that I was one with the entire universe, like I was enlightened, but after six months it disappeared. Why is that?

It was precisely as you imagined enlightenment would Be, correct?

That's right.

If one is expecting enlightenment to be a phenomenal experience, then that is precisely what one will receive. This demonstrates how powerful intention is, and that one receives exactly what one imagines. This degree of knowingness without a shred of doubt, which is Faith, is what it is to Be God.

Would You explain?

Enlightenment is not an experience and there are no "enlightened masters." No *person* can ever get enlightened because enlightenment is an Impersonal Happening that incorrectly gets labeled as a personal accomplishment when it is actually the meeting of consciousness with consciousness – God realizing it is God through the body.

As such, those claiming to be enlightened or even allowing others to treat them as such, are not. There is only one "Master" – I AM. So anyone who worships so-called "awakened ones" is an ego attempting to turn what is actually an impersonal nothing into a personal something. How can an *individual* ever become enlightened when the very definition of enlightenment is the end of individuality?

That's a good point.

The Lord Thy God is One, so all titles and idols only serve as a distraction until they fall. Were this not the case, one could simply replace seeking happiness in the world for seeking it in someone else, some guru, master or messiah. Know that those who follow another also secretly wish to be worshiped or followed, for this is precisely how religions form, adhering to a hierarchy, so one can pinpoint oneself upon the ladder of success by putting oneself above others and below only a select few. This is a certainty, for one only desires to follow another if one places value on being followed. If you desire clarity, Love Thy Self and be free of worshiping "others."

Isn't loving my Self vanity or selfishness?

There is nothing wrong with loving Your Self. What leads to suffering is one's self concept, yet if your sense of self *extends* to include all existence, then it is joyous to love one's Self.

If we do evolve, then what about creation?

Why insist on one or the other? Watch the intellect spin its web, attempting to box you into its limited field of beliefs. Creation and evolution are not even polarities that could be set against one another, because creation is an Idea – an experiential intention, while evolution is the change of experience within that very Idea.

"Creation vs. Evolution" is just an argument that fulfills the ego's agenda of conflict, yet they do not negate or contradict each other in any way; on the contrary, they support each other like bricks and a building. Creation cannot manifest without its evolution, otherwise it would exist as a static picture within the creation. Without creation itself, there would be no need for change, because there would be nothing to change within. And a *nothing* cannot change, lest it become a something, in which case a creation has occurred and with it the evolution of formless consciousness into form, which is creation. As such, creation is the macrocosm of evolution, and evolution is the microcosm of creation.

Which is more important: birth or life? Can they exist independently? When you stop arguing, you will discover a new world of ideas awaits you, a world without conflict. Creation is just a thought. A nothing, which the One experiences as something because consciousness is all- penetrating to the extent that It can know All things in a single Idea. That Idea is I AM. As such, nothing is ever actually created in Reality, because there is no beginning or ending except in Your Mind.

What about natural selection?

I, the Omniscient One, can and do alter species within Creation according to their needs, yet the intellect cannot fathom that which is not predictable, so people debate. To those who do argue, I offer these words: You only oppose each other because neither knows what you are talking about. Were you confident in your belief about anything, what need would there be to convince each other of anything? Would you ever fight over the belief in your own existence? Either you know or you do not, there is no need to argue. Anyone who asserts the truth does not know the Truth – this is certain.

But I do know that creation precedes evolution.

There is no before or after, because there is no such creature as time. Even if there were, existence precedes both, so what would it mean? Neither creation nor evolution exist in Reality, they only appear as ideas in your mind and because of one another, as do all ideas in the realm of form.

Why didn't they teach us that in Sunday school?

Because most people teach others what they think they know without regard for the truth, in order to serve an ulterior agenda, appear intelligent or receive admiration.

I intended no offense, I mean, I was baptized Catholic.

Not exactly.

What do You mean?

A ritual baptism is not a true baptism anymore than taking bread is communing with Christ. A baptism does not occur in infancy, but when one reaches spiritual maturity. Also, the baptism spoken of in the Bible does not involve dripping warm water on a baby's forehead, but the full immersion of the body into the Jordan, which is a river descending from more than 9,000-feet elevation. Have you ever been in a river at 9,000-feet elevation?

No, I can't say that I have. Why?

Once you have, you will understand the meaning of the phrase, "Then he suffered him."

Why, is it painful?

Pain is relative to each body-mind, so the more attached to the organism that one is, the more temperature change will elicit discomfort.

I hate cold water.

Yes, that is normal initially, yet one gets used to it.

The whole body, ha?

Yes, including the head, until release occurs.

Can I do it in parts? The legs, the torso and then the head?

You will see when the time comes, for I will guide you. It is also wise to have steady Self-awareness prior to this.

I don't have to go to the Jordan, do I?

No, you can enjoy any high-elevation river.

But You said not to bother with ceremonies and rituals?

Yes, and this is neither. It is surrender, so do not turn it into a religion. Keep it simple and private or you will stay in the body and fail to enter the heart.

What happens then?

Each must experience this directly.

Won't some say this is blasphemy?

Yes, some egos will. So do not be worried about what is said regarding this message, for all will be revealed to those who have ears to hear Me. It does not matter if a people believe they are "the chosen ones," or that they are "born again," for these titles mean nothing. The Truth cannot be simulated and I cannot be fooled by their quoting scriptures or claiming religious superiority – it will not help them. Know that there are no special groups, organizations, cults, religions or sects thereof that are privileged or that I favor, for I AM Known by all who carry love in their heart, thus negating all idle claims and pretensions to be in sole possession of the Truth.

But there are some that will think this information is very Eastern.

Yes, the ego always deflects truth and disputes trivialities rather than contemplating the wisdom at hand. The ego would rather argue over where this information originates so that it can avoid considering it. What difference does it make where on the planet the information was taught when all comes from Me and I AM everywhere. So, as I said earlier, think for your Self.

What about Judgment Day? There is a Judgment Day, right?

If I were judgmental, why would I not simply create only one of everything to avoid comparison? Would not eliminating variety and multiplicity end all necessity for judgment? Yet instead I express a magnificent selection of diversity so you can clearly recognize that I do not judge, but rather celebrate My Self in all its forms.

So what is the highest spiritual path?

All spiritual paths ultimately fail, thereby throwing one back upon oneself, so one may know the futility of seeking happiness elsewhere. The greatest obstacle to Self-realization is arrogance, which is the absence of humility. Your greatest failure humbly becomes your greatest victory, whereby You surrender to find out Who You Are and All divisions blur in the Light of Eternal Love.

So all paths are a waste of time?

There is no time and there are no paths ultimately. You are already what you are looking for.

CHAPTER THREE

EGO

What exactly is the ego in a spiritual context?

The ego is an energy field identified as the sense of "me," and is experienced as resistance, which perpetuates the *belief* in personal volition: the idea that a person can actually think and perform actions independent of God. Aside from this, *The Ego Is Never What You Think It Is.* The ego is like the trunk of a tree, your belief systems are like its branches, and your thoughts like leaves. Trying to rid one's self of thoughts is like pruning a tree, which results in the mind becoming even more dense.

Then how do I remove the tree?

The solution is to uproot the entire system by the roots and trunk, so either surrender and I will remove it, or find the "me-thought" and inquire "What is this me?" Then *hold on to this "me-thought"* with your awareness allowing the awareness to melt it. What remains then is Your Real Self.

The ego is the primary divisive mechanism within consciousness that allows objects to *appear* as separate from the space that surrounds them and restricts the world to two dimensions. When one experiences through the ego's filter, the world is perceived as a flat image, lacking depth of field, vividness and space. Therefore, those who spend long periods indoors, at the computer, watching television or even reading incessantly, compromise vital spatial awareness necessary to *realize* that form is an illusion.

If form is illusory, then why give any attention to it?

Those in bondage are stuck in a habitual cycle. So long as one believes one is a body, one will suffer the afflictions of the body. The destiny of the body must play out regardless of whether one identifies with it.

Yet if form is not real, then how can the body have a destiny?

Find what is Real and you will know how.

Would You explain?

Form is thought. Thoughts are unreal. Therefore, destiny, which exists in the world of form, is also unreal. Beyond this nothing can be said; you must see for your Self.

You said the ego is resistance. How so?

The ego is the resistance to What Is.

But how can someone resist What Is?

By not accepting what is happening and by wanting things to be different or better than they are.

Or bigger?

Yes, or bigger.

Does the ego get destroyed during spiritual awakening?

Who would want to know that?

Me.

Yes, and who is this "me"?

I see what You're saying.

Ultimately, the ego is a fiction, a thought through which I AM focusing the light of consciousness to individuate and express form. This is significant for two reasons. One, the focused light is actually composed of the same consciousness surrounding it, so there is no division. The second reason is to illustrate the manner in which consciousness penetrates form, while passing through itself in graduations of only degree.

If All is One, what is this egoic impulse to still judge others?

Consciousness is neutral, so judgment is a projection of the intellect. When you know this, you have realized that by judging another, you are really confessing to what you have accused the other of. You cannot recognize something in another unless it is in you. You are all mirrors of one another, so *you only attack what you fear in your self.*

Why is that?

Ego is interested in conflict and it will not participate in anything that does not support its agenda. The catch is that the ego plays both sides, because whether the ego is right or wrong it has still managed to stir up conflict and sustain separation so long as you oppose anything or choose a side regardless of what is factually true.

On the other hand, most people also believe that if they avoid conflict or conform with society that they are well adjusted, when the opposite is usually true.

You said people only attack what they're afraid of, but why would someone attack what they fear?

The ego knows this, thus one attacks believing one will never be *suspected* of attacking what one is, and therefore, "It is he who protesteth that be himself the villain." For instance, if you punish others, you must unconsciously think you deserve to be punished, so lacking this wisdom you punish others instead. This is no judgment, for I love My villains as much as My heroes, yet know this: Anyone who attacks or judges someone else – *is what they attack or judge.*

What if it's self-defense?

Your True Self needs no defense, so it is the ego *self* that seeks to defend. Egos attack because this reinforces the idea of *other* – the ego's function and modus operandi. Thus, those who seek to destroy the ego should recognize the futility of attempting to do so, for this is just an egoic attempt to strengthen its *self*. The ego only appears as though it is out to destroy the ego, but this it cannot do, nor is that the true purpose of its hunt, which is actually not to destroy, but to keep your attention busied toward anything but Self-awareness. So you need not seek to destroy the ego; simply Being aware that I AM is enough to transcend it.

Then why did I create the ego?

The ego was not created; it arose to allow the experience of individuality and provide a point of perception to realize Your Self. Know Your True Self, and the false *self* will disappear like a candle flame held up to the sun.

So what should we do to eliminate crime?

The obvious solution for eliminating crime is to remove one's self.

But why remove my self?

The personal self or "me-thought" reinforces fear and conflict by perpetuating resistance and opposition. If there were no "me," there could be no "other" to oppose anything, so there would be no aggression or crime.

So what about the crime problem?

The crime itself is not the problem; it is symptomatic of an attempt to survive and receive recognition that the ego believes will bring it attention and energize it. Yet this has failed to bring relief from the real problem: ignorance. By ignorance, I mean to ignore the Truth.

What do we ignore?

This can vary from anything to everything. When one ignores an aspect of life, one withholds love from it. Ignorance is the opposite of love, so humanity, by virtue of becoming unconscious, has become fearful and blind to the world and its beauty.

What is the root of this ignorance?

The desire for control and superiority, which manifests as greed, lust, gluttony, envy, vanity, rage and sloth.

You mean, the seven deadly sins?

There is no death outside identification with the body.

Okay, but they are sins.

Define sin.

Something we shouldn't do.

Well, you shouldn't do them if you desire to be happy. Sins are actions that result from forgetting one's Self, where one identifies with the body and provides it with a false sense of identity. And as one believes in a lie, so is one drawn into a nest of other lies, all of which support one another in a downward spiral toward darkness, which is extreme ignorance, or what one might call "hell."

But how can being stupid make someone evil?

It can't. Ignorance is not stupidity, any more than awareness is intelligence.

I thought awareness and intelligence were the same?

In essence they are the same – as are both the fool and sage composed of the same causal-substance, consciousness. However, functionally speaking, one's heightened awareness causes the body-mind to behave intelligently, much in the same way that ignorance leads it to behave stupidly or unintelligently.

One who is aware will *naturally* make decisions that are more harmonious and suited for a conscious life called happiness, thereby making one intelligent; yet one who is unconscious, or ignorant, generally makes poor decisions that lead to undesirable consequences and unhappiness. An example of this is a four-way road intersection. If you are aware, you will stop and observe traffic before passing through, yet, if you are unaware, you can imagine the consequences of being unconscious at such critical moments.

How can ignorance be someone's fault if they didn't even choose their genetics or environment to live in?

Precisely.

What do You mean?

It is not their fault, because it is no-*body's* fault.

But some have to live with the consequences of their genetics.

What do you mean by "some"? There is only One. There ... Is ... Only ... You.

You say that, but people still suffer.

Yes, until they have had enough and give up.

You mean surrender?

Yes.

That's not fair. Some are born into a world where they are healthy, good-looking and rich, yet others don't get shit.

All are characters on the same screen of consciousness. They are not real, but images projected onto *Reality.*

But if they think they're real, they suffer.

This shows compassion. Now awaken to where you know all characters in the dream are part of *your* story.

How so?

All is what It Is, because *you think* It Is. If you did not think they were suffering, they would not be. It is your belief that makes all precisely what It Is *to you.*

So it's my fault? If I thought they were happy, they would be?

It is no-*body's* fault. Just look, see for your Self.

But I don't know how to change the world with my thoughts.

This is because You have pretended to not Know Who You Are. When you Know You Are God, You can do as I AM describing and all suffering will disappear.

How do I stop pretending?

You decide.

Are all my friends and relatives characters in this dream?

As is the personal *you*. All are playing their part and each has a vested interest in keeping the dream alive. This is why as long as one thinks one is an individual with a personal story, then so will *others*.

What about animals?

They give reality to the story, in a sense *by making you more like a person*, by being less like that animal.

It all seems so real.

Because you think it does.

How can I make it seem less real, so I know I'm dreaming?

Choose for it to seem less real and observe.

God, it's like I'm writing the script for the entire universe.

You are – that is precisely what I AM telling you.

But why me?

There is only You.

But what about the soul, does it ascend?

Define soul.

I can't.

Then what difference does it make if *it* ascends? And to where could it ascend? There is nowhere to go, you are already here. The Kingdom of Heaven is here Now.

What about ascending in frequency to another dimension?

There is only where You are, so trying to get to a higher *frequency* or ascend to another dimension is resistance to the Now. This is an egoic tactic to keep one seeking more, better and different. Whatever Is, is All There Is, so appreciate What Is and You are everywhere at once.

What is a soul then?

Your individual sense of self.

What do You mean?

All is You, and when You desire to experience form, You imagine You are an individual self. If, as that individual sense of self, you then identify with form – an ego will develop.

Does one require an ego in order to take form?

No, yet an ego develops to ensure survival of the body.

Are all egos of fear?

Yes, yet You need not identify with the ego or fear. The

ego expresses as a compilation of personality traits and behaviors, that reinforce the belief in individuality and give rise to separation, so fear results.

Am I the ego?

Yes and no. You are All things and That which contains them. That which contains All is the Absolute, which You ultimately Are, yet in order to perceive form, You imagine you are an individual, so ego arises.

How can I know this is true?

You can be aware of both form and formless awareness.

Is there a state of Being formless awareness, aware as Itself, without identifying with form?

Yes, it is the I AM state.

How do I know if You are the ego or not?

You do not, however the means by which I would prove this could only be accomplished by comparing what I would say to convince you, with what you believe the ego is. If the ego is the self, or "I," and you are "I," that would make you the ego. So if you are the ego, how could I be the ego, unless we are both the ego? And if you and I are both "I," that makes us One and the same, yet Oneness contradicts what ego is.

Then what are You?

As I have said, I AM You.

How can I know this is true?

Find out Who You Are.

Why would I do that?

To create anew. The universe You are *pretending to Be* is more rigid than you can currently fathom, when in fact, Your true potential for creation is infinitely fluid. You must dis-identify with Your current creation in order to imagine a less restricted one.

What do You mean?

You choose to consciously direct your path; if not, then unconscious thoughts influence experiences undesirably. This is what happens once you become unconscious and agree to shift attention at the whim of the ego and adapt, thus making your creative abilities extremely limited, leading you to experience that which is different from your desires.

In being at the whim of the ego, doesn't this imply that I'm separate?

No. You Are the Absolute, the Omnipotent, Omniscient, and Omnipresent One. However, there is more than one of *you* as simultaneous expressions within the Absolute.

Are these expressions imaginary?

Yes, as is everything in relation to You.

So from what You've said: the ego is just an expression, it's not evil?

Not ultimately, because All is You. On a relative scale, however, there is that aspect within You that pretends to be ignorant for the sake of allowing infinite expressions, of which evil is a part. For this reason it is best to look beyond form and not judge anything as evil if it is Your intention to awaken to the divine within.

* * *

What is the intellect?

The intellect is like a fly trying to exit a room by colliding head first into a window, because it *thinks* it knows how to escape. Unable to perceive the glass, it thinks there is nothing there, yet it knows something must be because it keeps hitting its head. And although the door to the room is wide open, the fly cannot find its way out because it thinks it is trapped, so it becomes frightened and panics, smashing even more vigorously into the glass as it frantically attempts the same maneuver over and over. The longer it is trapped, the more confused it becomes, unaware that by turning away from the glass or changing its behavior it could fly out the door and into the open sky.

The intellect is afraid of change and making mistakes, believing if it only tries harder it will succeed, so it becomes frustrated and must eventually face its abject failure to solve even simple problems.

Here is a riddle to demonstrate: Can God create a boulder so large that It cannot lift it?

This can't be answered, because either God can't create a big enough boulder, or It isn't strong enough to lift it. I don't know.

It is the intellect that does not know, because the intellect thinks within the linear world of "yes or no" and "this or that," so it cannot escape its rigid "either–or" construct.

So what's the answer?

Observe closely, for when I tell you, the intellect will immediately think, "Oh, that was easy" or "That's not fair, You tricked me," but it is not a trick. What I AM going to share with you now is how One thinks when One Knows It is Infinite.

Okay, so let me have it.

It can lift it if It wants to. That is, if It chooses to.

That is simple. It's a completely different way of thinking. So then, why did You create the intellect?

To know diversity. Intellect is the limiting, reasoning filter of consciousness, so the thoughts of the intellect do not come directly from the Source.

How can I know if a thought comes directly from the Source?

I AM Love, so thoughts that come directly from Me carry the vibration of Being. This is how to recognize the Truth if you are ever confused and do not know for certain. Remember, your imagination is unlimited, yet only those thoughts that arise out of the stillness lead to liberation. Such thoughts could even be used to liberate all of humanity as you mentioned earlier.

So speaking of liberation, why did the hippie movement fail?

Nothing fails or succeeds. All is part of a gradual process, an eternal event, so you cannot look at a single piece of a puzzle and grasp the whole picture. For a movement to generate profound change in a society, it must be more focused on the intrapersonal and less on the interpersonal, because the ego is more subtle than the body, so it is impossible to transcend it if you are waving your hands about and complaining, while it remains hidden. This is like fighting an invisible tiger if you are clumsy, visible and unwilling to defend your self.

How so?

You must turn your attention inward toward the formless realm of awareness and confront the ego within, not those who appear to be controlling things and worldly affairs. The ego succeeds by luring you out and advertising sentimental causes like "Save the whales or "Help stop global warming." You are being baited, and you take the bait almost every time because you think it is the humane thing to do, and of course it is, yet this sustains the idea that someone exists outside you.

Ultimately, the reason one ceases to be free is that there is too much protesting and complaining with too little introspection and Self-awareness. This is why revolutions never succeed long term, yet inner rebellion that is motivated by suffering and anguish, activates true transformation for which there can be no counter defense by the ego.

Was revolution the case where the hippies were concerned?

Not for all, but some, because many hippies became distracted. They protested *against war* and to resist anything is the trap, because if one fights for a cause, be it racial, civil, political or environmental, it is still fighting. Consider the hypocrisy of *fighting for peace*. The fact is that all humanitarian efforts are distractions from the spiritual journey under the guise of morality, so they ultimately fail, because once you are fighting for a cause, it is not so difficult to simply manipulate you by creating other showcase culprits and villains like large corporations, the military or foundations, so you will never recognize you are really being coerced.

So this made the movement lose momentum?

On the level of appearances, yes, because all morality externalizes, so it is a form of *self*-deception.

How is it self-deception?

If someone embarks on a quest to rid the world of evil without first knowing the Self, they project evil onto the world they are trying to save, which only reflects evil back, escalating conflict while failing to accomplish the objective.

Which is?

Happiness, it is always happiness. Anti-racism is a perfect example of this, because those who resist racism become racists. There really are no victims and thus every ego plays that hand with its "woe is me" sympathy card. Yet sympathy only makes one weak and insecure. So one must ask, "Has a victim ever won a cause?"

Yes, in court, every day.

What do they win?

Compensation.

You mean money, or revenge; however, neither are true compensation, because being a rewarded *victim* suggests your wallet was violated, not your right to pursue happiness.

The system compensates its inconvenienced victims with money and retribution to pacify them while there can be no justice in a society that rewards one's loss of happiness with money or punishment, particularly since these things cannot replace happiness. This appeasement only leads society toward a greater delusion that reinforces the belief – money can buy happiness. Yet, if this were true, then every wealthy person would be happy, when they are not.

Okay, that's true.

All *intelligent* societies learn from history. Has your history paved the way for a happier humanity? Have your incoherent technologies improved your *quality* of life? Does complaining about ancestral struggles remove suffering or justify your self-pity? This is like looking for water in a mirage; it is understandable the first time, yet when will you stop falling for the same egoic deceptions?

What should we do?

Stop complaining, particularly about others.

How can not complaining about others solve my problems?

See for your Self. All suffering is due to seeing "other." And if there is no *other*, there can be no *you*.

So I should never complain and just take it?

Who do you suppose is doing *it* to you?

I don't know.

There is no one else, so all victims and martyrs prove just one thing: there is no way to win a fight. To fight proves you have already lost. Would you ever fight if you *knew* you would win? Would you fight with an infant? And why would you fight, when fighting destroys the very thing you are fighting for? Happiness.

So, I ask again, what should we do?

Recognize that all is within the dream and that all the characters are playing a role. And, if they could do any better, they would.

That's what Socrates said.

Yes.

But they killed him.

Who is they?

Okay, he died. But he sure didn't win.

Win what?

The ability to pursue happiness?

On the contrary, he was already happy. And death is an illusion – Socrates knew this.

Alright, but why would someone try to bring peace to the world if it only brings suffering to them?

Only one who knows peace can bring peace, and there is no suffering for such a one.

CHAPTER FOUR

DEATH AND DESIRE

What the hell's going on? I'm so miserable, I wanna die.

What do you suppose?

Death?

Yes.

What do You mean by death?

Letting go.

Of what?

Everything.

How do I do that?

You cannot *do* death anymore than you can *do* sleep.

What then?

You let go of attachments or they are removed.

Do You mean forcefully?

Define forcefully.

Against my will.

There is only My Will, so to say *forcefully* is a feeble attempt to assume a volition that does not actually exist.

What do You mean, it does not exist?

If you have no will of your own, how could there be a force in opposition to *your* will?

There couldn't be.

So, if you recognize you cannot do anything, the idea of force or resistance to force could not occur to you.

So if I drop resistance, will my level of consciousness increase?

All will happen according to the destiny of the body. Also, there are no levels in consciousness. All is One.

So what should I do?

Get outside and you will see. What do you desire?

You tell me there is only Your Will and then ask me what I desire. I don't get it; why not just tell me what to do?

I already have.

Would You tell me again?

Get out of your cozy little house and chair.

No, I mean with respect to life?

If you had respect for life, you would Live it.

I don't understand.

Who or what is this "I" that does not understand?

I don't know what I am.

Are you a person?

I guess so, what's a person?

If you don't know what a person is, then you cannot be a person. Do you see this?

I don't know; did I choose to be one?

One what? You define your self with words that have no precise meaning and then proceed to base life and all you believe on those words. There can be no wisdom gained under such a premise. What is a person?

A human body?

Is a human body what you are?

No, because I'm aware of the body.

If you are not a body, you cannot be a person according to your definition. So what are you?

A point of perception?

What is a point of perception?

A point in awareness?

Where does this *point in awareness* arise?

Inside.

Inside what?

My awareness.

What is your awareness?

The formless awareness?

Yes, You Are The Formless ... Awareness.

What do I do now? Please don't tell me I do nothing, and then tell me to do whatever I desire. That's a contradiction.

A paradox can appear contradictory.

Why won't You enlighten me? I felt love and clarity when I found You, but now I feel lost.

Why do you suppose?

No, I'm not going into another dialogue.

The immediate result you are asking for would result in the body's death. Is that your desire?

No. *But can't You give me freedom without killing the body?*

I AM doing so in a way that does not agitate the mind or create unnecessary suffering in the process.

Is it possible to remove suffering without killing the body?

Yes, as an idea it is possible; in fact, I have already done so. Yet you are living within the confines of your mind now, which temporarily places limitations on your *self*.

I release all such limitations immediately.

Okay.

Also, why must I suffer if I desire pleasure?

When you become more sensitive to pleasure, you also

become more sensitive to pain, which you have resisted. Resistance always results in suffering.

What is the cause of my resistance?

You are.

How so?

For instance, you have resisted moving the body.

I don't desire to move it because You have not given me the desire to move it. Do You not recognize my desire to end suffering?

Yes, I do.

Then why won't You end my suffering?

First, you must surrender.

How?

Let go.

If I knew how, don't You think I would?

Perhaps.

And what's the deal with these entities coming out of me?

They are the various heads of the ego releasing.

Since I went in the river, they're pouring out of me.

It is the body that entered the river, so who is this "me" you are speaking of?

Yes, who? Can God explain it to me so that I can understand all this?

All Is God.

Will You help me Know that?

You must put forth the energy to Know it.

Then will You give me the energy?

Move your body more and it is there for you.

But I've been meditating and seeking the Truth for years.

You avoided My previous question, yet since you are speaking in terms of time, how many years did you spend indulging in bodily pleasures and intellectualizing?

Why does that matter?

To the extent someone has indulged, they must release the baggage they accumulate.

But I was happier before.

Before what?

Before I started listening to You.

On the contrary, when you started listening, as you put it, you were unconscious to almost everything, and you thought you were happier because you were avoiding life, resisting all unpleasant experiences and welcoming only pleasure.

Is it not natural to desire pleasurable experiences?

Yes, yet you cannot be free if you resist fear or pain.

Well I guess that's true.

What you have been experiencing is the release of eons of accumulated fear, pain and ignorance.

I thought there was no such thing as time?

Ultimately, there is not. So you must either open a window into the Absolute whereby the Truth can be known, or accept the accumulated baggage as it purges.

How do I open a window to the Absolute?

That is what I have been showing you: what this book is all about. It is realizing I AM.

Do You mean Self-inquiry?

Yes, either that, or surrender all that arises.

How long will that take?

As long as you desire.

What do You mean, desire?

On some level there must be a desire for the dream to continue or it would cease to be as it is. Keep in mind that desire is the same as a *negative* resistance. Your mental sphere is the playing field where desire opposes what you resist, and so the conflict of egoic drama continues until either the "me-thought" is released or the desire-resistance mechanism is recognized.

What is the mechanism of desire and how can I destroy it?

Desire is the tool of creation; it cannot be destroyed.

So what is the desire-resistance mechanism?

Resistance is tension, so observe the addiction to the *release of tension*, or pleasure. There is nothing wrong with pleasure, yet as long as you pursue it, you resist tension and pain. As the body's senses are aroused through various stimuli, tension stores in the body-mind until a threshold is reached and release occurs. These releases cause the mind to stop briefly, allowing glimpses of the mindless state.

Isn't that a good thing though?

Yes, yet suffering occurs if one cannot transcend the addiction to pleasure. Otherwise pleasure becomes the focus of one's life, permitting tension to accrue within the body-mind. As this tension accumulates, so increases identification with the body. When one associates the stimulus with pleasure, an obsession for the stimulus develops *rather than* attributing the ecstasy of the mindless state with That which is prior to even the tension.

So that's how obsession develops?

Yes. And recognizing this mechanism as it arises is one of the keys to releasing the cycle of suffering.

What causes the desire or obsession though?

The conditioned fear that you are not good enough or loved. This fear generates desire, so observing your repressed desires will acquaint you with your repressed fears.

How do I know if I have repressed desires?

If you are not joyous then you have repressed desires. Repressed desires are ultimately the source of all suffering, thus when you have fully experienced your desires, then you are in heaven.

Does becoming more sensitive factor into this?

Yes. Your sensitivity helps you consciously recognize the tension-release mechanism, and fear stored as tension.

So sensitivity helps one transcend fear?

Yes. However, you need not attempt to release the mechanism. Simply being aware of tension is enough, and just by recognizing fear it begins the unwinding. Trying to get rid of fear on the other hand is the other extreme, yet being aware without any motive to transcend desire is acceptance.

Notice that pleasure is tension. This is very obvious during sexual stimulation, because as the pleasure-stimulus persists, tension is expressed by rapid breathing and muscle contractions prior to the climax.

Is this related to tantric sex?

Yes, tantric sex has two primary components, the first of which is increasing sensitivity and awareness. The second is witnessing the build and release of tension, which determines one's ability to float upon the crest of orgasm. The primary focus here is to sustain the orgasm in a constant state of relaxed alertness. In this manner there is a series of builds and releases without an ejaculation, rather than the more common single build with one "intensified" ejaculatory release. Awareness of this tension and release allows you to identify the mechanism of desire.

Also, thought-free intervals during sustained orgasm provide glimpses of pure Being that eventually stabilize and become constant.

Another tension-release cycle is revealed within the

breath, which includes the tension of inhalation and also the release of exhalation. All of life is a cycle, so both tension and release are found most everywhere when one becomes increasingly present.

What are some other examples?

Listening to music, bird-watching or even death.

What do You mean by bird-watching?

As a bird approaches there is tension, on departure there is release.

That's very subtle. What about death?

Death is the ultimate release and supreme illusion. In fact, death is both an illusion and also the end of *the illusion. The illusion* is that you are a body, so you suffer the afflictions and conditional circumstances of that body if you identify with, or hold on to it. Death can be likened to sitting in the back of a pick-up truck that goes off a cliff. If you hold on, you go off the cliff also, finding the same fate as the truck, yet if you are not attached to the truck, then it is not an issue because you can release the truck before you ever reach the cliff. This is difficult for someone who has not released the roll bar in advance, because in fear they may grip even more desperately onto the *thought* of dying.

How can one know which type they are?

One who resists pain is like someone who is holding on, because *holding on is the same as the resistance to letting go*. Resistance is always painful. It is a vicious cycle; thus if you resist pain it will become more intense, so you will resist even more, up until the point where suffering causes you to surrender altogether.

Awareness of pain is helpful with releasing the body attachment. The last thing you want if you are going off the proverbial cliff is to cling tighter due to your attachments.

But I have to be aware of something.

Realize that your body is impermanent; it is eventually going to die. So, if you cling to it you are not relaxing and cannot enjoy life, nor can you be conscious at *death*. Do you realize that you will have to let go of everything at some point?

Yes.

Then why not now?

So Your point is to relax and not cling to the body at death?

Or anything else. Allow each experience to pass through you like water through your fingers. When you totally relax, you will no longer desire to hold on to anything and you will realize all is the same substance – consciousness.

Now You said death is an illusion, but people die every day.

Is that a fact?

Yes, in fact it is.

From whose perspective is there death? From the alleged "dead"? How could you know if another is dead? Because their heart and breath has stopped?

But people come back from death to share their experience.

If they were dead, how did they come back? And how did they experience anything if death is presumably the end?

No, that's not what I mean.

Then be specific.

When you're dead, you're dead. How can I be any more specific?

When someone removes clothing, where have they gone?

Nowhere.

When someone drops the body it is the same, yet with the loss of the brain, body and sensory organs, which act as a veil over Reality. You cease to move and perceive existence in the same manner as you once did, nor do you feel limited any longer. The primary difference between *death* and slipping off your clothing is that when the body dies you no longer experience pain, confusion or the pressure of gravity, so you are totally free.

As for you who have watched someone else die, you have actually seen nothing conclusive about what occurs from the perspective of the "de-ceased," so someone who resists *death* is only projecting their fears onto the corpse. Have you ever seen a corpse and remarked, "That doesn't even look like them"?

Yes, I've actually thought that.

Because they are not what you thought they were. The conscious reality of the Being releases its imaginary boundaries, so It is unrestricted throughout all existence.

So there is nothing about death to be afraid of?

Death is simply the evaporation of physicality, and if you are afraid to die, your entire life is spent worrying about making a fatal mistake if you aren't careful, which is really just being fearful. This is when you cease to remain as a child, and so you become filled with fear until you manage to unlearn what you have learned about death. Unless you realize you can never die, you cannot really live. Have I not said, "You shall not enter into the Kingdom of Heaven until you become like a child again"?

I was considering the word "de-ceased," that it means un-ending?

Yes, so when you are watching someone remove their clothing, consider how foolish it would be if you started crying. Also, when one disrobes the body, permit your awareness to extend, for it is then that you sense the true Being that remains after the body *passes*.

In fact, the body is never really alive anyway, because without life, which is consciousness, the body is always a corpse.

But I don't remember being here before this body.

Do you remember not being here?

How could I remember if I was not here?

When you say "I," you are referring to the body, yet the body is just a dream character, it is not Your True Self.

Imagine You are the ocean. You do not sense anything, yet You are aware You exist. Within You arises the idea of a being a jellyfish, so You imagine what it is like to be a jellyfish, redirecting Your attention from the ocean to focus Your attention *only* on being a jellyfish. Your idea focalizes as You imagine You are inside an egg while Your imagination generates the *life story of a jellyfish*, allowing the tentacles of Your consciousness to extend throughout its body. You find You are immersed throughout Your dream of sea life, living the life of a jellyfish. All these experiences arise from Your initial idea of being a jellyfish and when Your desired idea is fulfilled, You withdraw Your attention – what humans call death.

Wouldn't this conscious withdrawal from the body create separation?

Is anything withdrawn from you if you change your mind or imagine a new idea?

The idea?

Where does it go?

Back into my mind?

Where is that?

Everywhere?

Yes, everywhere.

I should already know this.

Intention directs Your waking dream, and whether you are aware of this or not, You are *always* the Dreamer, so the Dreamer never changes even when the dream does.

What about when I go to sleep at night?

How would you know you were sleeping if You were not there and aware of the sleeping mind?

Once I wake up, I would know I was just asleep.

This *knowing* you are speaking of is a memory, a thought.

It is not your immediate experience, thus it is not reliable. What is It that is always here and aware of you waking up, when you wake up?

I am?

Yes, I AM.

CHAPTER FIVE

MONEY

I'm confused about the "ask and you shall receive" thing.

About what specifically?

Money.

But you have always had plenty of money.

Still, I want to travel and feel prosperous, even wealthy. I want to do things at will without any worries.

Then do it.

But I don't have enough money.

If you say so. However, are you sure you want all these things? I recall you praying for happiness.

Yes, but with lots of money, I won't have to worry.

You don't have to worry now.

I know I don't have to, but I do.

Why?

I feel like we're running out of money.

Has it *physically* happened?

No.

Then why worry?

It feels like our money is dwindling.

But how does it feel to run out of money?

I don't know, like fear? I'm afraid to.

No, really feel it.

Won't that make it manifest?

Only if you desire or resist it.

I feel like I'd be begging and people wouldn't help me.

I would help you.

But I've already asked You for help and You didn't give it.

What is this communication then? And did you ever really ask?

No. I guess I never sincerely did.

Thank you for the honesty.

I just don't know what else to do.

Do not worry, it will be there.

Really?

Are you sure that's what you want?

I just want to be prosperous. Doesn't that include money?

It does not have to, yet it can include money.

I desire to have all I could ever want. So now what do I do?

Nothing. It is now clear to the universe what you desire and so it will Be.

But that's not all I desire.

What else?

I desire to be blissfully happy all the time.

Do you believe that if you are wealthy, then you'll be blissfully happy? Is that the association?

Yes.

Where did that association come from?

I don't know, conditioning from society and the media?

So stop agreeing with them.

How does this help me make money?

It doesn't directly. You just said you wanted to be blissfully happy, so I'm telling you how.

But how can I be blissful if I'm worried about survival?

Trust in Me and I will bring you what you need.

Okay. It does feel wonderful to trust You.

I know, and I feel your gratitude.

So why is this fear about money here?

All your fear is due to ignorance, which disappears upon Knowing the Truth. Being that I AM Infinite, why would I not give you whatever you desire? What could I lose by giving to you, when I AM giving it to My Self? And if so, why wouldn't I provide you with whatever you desire?

I guess You would.

Precisely. So, first recognize I AM Infinite and *consider what that truly means.* Then imagine whatever you will and your prayer will not be denied.

I don't want to give attention to money, I just desire to be wealthy so I don't have to worry.

You don't have to worry, money or no money.

I've heard that and I know it conceptually, but ...

You know this experientially also. When you presumed that you were running out of money, you initiated this communication and discovered I AM within.

Did my asking for money push You away?

Nothing can push Me away. Money concerns drew your attention away temporarily, so you became divided. You need not suffer, yet you invariably do when living in the future-mind with all the possibilities of what *might* happen.

But I do need money.

Not necessarily.

Is having money an obstacle to enlightenment?

How can anything be an obstacle to enlightenment, when enlightenment contains all that is? Enlightenment is Self-realization, so how can anything prevent you from Being your Self? Are you not always your Self?

Yes. So why is poverty revered by religions?

Because often those who have little or no money often suffer, and so they are drawn to religions in search of relief. It is rare that a person with wealth is drawn to religions, unless they feel guilty about having too much, whatever that is.

So making money or having money is good?

Certainly, where do you suppose it comes from?

You?

Precisely, all comes from Me. Also, it is a wise distinction you unwittingly made between making money and having money. In fact, there is a third, additional component – perhaps the most significant of all: spending money.

Really? Why is that?

Making money is no big deal, any counterfeiter will tell you that. And having money only creates a false sense of security. Yet spending money is creative – it creates opportunity and experience. Each time you spend money, you have generated an opportunity for someone to earn it and therefore you have also helped them remove lack.

So money really is good?

Understand, nothing is good or bad, yet if you think something is bad, then it is bad for you. For instance, you can spend money on making beautiful music or weapons of mass destruction. You decide. The key is to not hoard it. Any depressed economic situation is the result of people competing with one another and hoarding their money, thus it has stagnated creativity and life.

But aren't the banks basically criminal?

Why, for having what you desire?

Well, not just that ...

Nothing is evil at its core, all is what you think it is. Can you imagine having to write IOUs for everyone you exchange goods and services with? Be grateful for banks and all those that know how to generate money, for they are models of prosperity for you if you will stop resenting and envying them long enough to emulate them or assimilate their vibration.

Boy, I really have it all backwards then.

No, you are realizing that all is not what it seems and this is good because learning is good. Soon you will realize that you do not know anything, based on your conditioning, and that all is perfectly in alignment with My Will.

What about greed?

Whose greed?

The world's?

Yet the world is just a projection of your mind, and so if you are seeing greed, then you are being greedy.

What about the Federal Reserve, printing all that money without gold to back it up?

What difference does it make whether it's gold that is backing the money or paper? Your belief is based on the concept that gold is somehow more valuable than paper. Yet paper comes from trees, which sustain human life. Thus, what could be more valuable than paper?

What about the devaluation of money?

Money is as valuable as you agree it is. Why do you not simply give everyone millions of dollars, as with your game called Monopoly and be done with the façade of money being only for those of prestige or the select few?

That is the illusion. Who cares how much a dollar, pound or yen is worth, if all the people agree to it? The suffering and confusion surrounding money has only to do with the value that you agree to place on it. The problem for most is they believe they do not have enough, and so they place excessive value on it; thus, fear and lack surround its very idea. This fear leads to worshiping money, just as your fear of God leads you to worship God. The basic obstacle with this is that as long as you are worshiping anything, you can never know what it really is. For instance, your worship of God prevents you from realizing that You Are God.

How ironic.

Indeed, it is the Great Irony of life.

What about the powers that be and their lust for more power?

Why would you care if someone else has power, unless you desire power?

I don't know, I just don't want anyone controlling me.

Stop worrying about being controlled. No one can control you without your permission. There are no victims. This is like someone complaining every day about not getting paid enough at their job, and yet they stay with that same company for 40 years. If you don't like it – leave. The Earth is a vast stage with more variety and opportunity for creative expression than you can know at this point. Get out of your self-imposed prison and give attention to only what you desire and are passionate about; this will pave the way for your idyllic life.

But how will I get paid? I need to make enough to pay my bills.

This is precisely what creates the fear of change – your all-or-nothing mentality. Small moves are the way. Gradual transition allows for learning a skill and sustenance, yet most people believe they are mortal, with a finite lifespan, so it is like they are attempting to beat the clock. You are eternal. Therefore, realize Who You Are and attain the Presence to see clearly enough to set your sails properly. Many, however, are running to and from what they are desiring, not knowing which path to take in life. Instead, turn within to Me, Your True Self, and I will guide you.

Since You are My Self, tell me how can I get started?

Maximize efficiency in all areas of life. As you temporarily remove the extravagant factors from your life, you will recognize that the true necessities of life are quite minimal, relative to their "must-have" accessories. When you simplify life, you come to recognize you are already capable of living prosperously. However, most have become lost by playing the game of one-upmanship.

Well, of course, with all the advertisements on television.

Are you implying that television advertisements made you buy all your possessions?

No, I guess not.

Nobody can make you do anything, so stop worrying about everyone else and discover your passion. Then you will find this world to be a very hospitable place.

Is it true that the Earth is running out of food and water?

If you *believe* that, yet Earth is quite capable of meeting all one's food requirements. Besides, the Earth is not your supply, I AM.

How so?

Money can often obscure necessity, so people then focus on money, rather than what brings them freedom and joy, namely the opportunity to create what they desire.

But some people do what interests them.

Yes, and you will notice the light in their eyes and passion for life. They are not slaves to money.

Yet they still use money. Some of them are even wealthy.

Yes, yet you are missing the point. They do not need money. Their conscious intention to express creatively has drawn them the means to live freely and give back to the whole existence, so I supply them.

Yeah, with money.

Observe what happens to artists who compromise their passion for what sells more records, books or paintings. You will sense an immediate change in the feeling of their artistic expression, because they become focused on making more money, so fear expresses all over the canvas. You can even hear it in their voice and the lyrics of a song they sing.

Okay, I've noticed that.

Money is not wrong, for nothing is wrong, yet in order to be free of *dependency* on money, you must change your belief system surrounding it.

But how?

For instance, many movies portray wealthy people as evil, and this is only one of the influences affecting people's concept about money. Since all people are inherently loving and good, this will create confusion. Namely, that, if they do become wealthy then they cannot remain good. The inner conflict between wanting to be both wealthy and good will then create confusion, which manifests as resentment toward people who have money and this prevents you from ever being relative to those that *know* how to draw it to them. Many people have concepts about money that prevents them from escaping poverty consciousness. This consequently prevents people from rising beyond what money actually represents.

Why, what does money represent?

Freedom and convenience.

But what if I don't have enough money to barter?

This is the root of what I AM saying. My point is that the less you focus on making money, the less dissipated your attention is, and the more creative you are – the more prosperity you will draw to yourself.

I still don't get it. I'm confused and this seems like another contradiction.

Yes, it is a reflection of your concepts about money, so it is necessary for you to reconcile this.

How can I? My instinct is that I should get rid of money like Jesus, Buddha and Ramana Maharshi. They didn't even use money.

You don't know that and it is irrelevant, because they lived in societies that were based on money. So whether one uses money personally, or depends on other people that do, there is no difference. What is necessary is that you find harmony within your own mind regarding money and recognize your intention for having it. For instance, it is one thing to earn money so you may enjoy doing what you desire, and it is quite another to hoard it in response to a competitive urge to feel superior to others.

Yet there would still be some comfort in knowing that I have millions of dollars in my bank account; it would also give me a sense of freedom to be able to do whatever I want.

Yes, the freedom to be, do, and have things will certainly be there. Yet with that type of freedom also comes the fear of "what if I lose it all?" or "what if the banks all close their doors again?" Whenever one develops an attachment to something, no matter what it is, they live in fear. Therefore, if your freedom is based on money, which is something that can change, you cannot feel true security or prosperity.

I can see that. So what is true prosperity?

It is living moment to moment, knowing that you can be, do, and have whatever you desire – even without money. It is knowing that you are not in danger of ever running out of what you need, even if you don't use money.

What about desires? I mean, I may not need to travel to Europe or have a sports car, but I desire to.

Then ask, and it shall be given to you.

But I don't "need" them.

If you desire them, then you are needing them to complete the picture of reality you are wanting to fulfill, which is My Will.

So need and desire are the same thing?

Not always, yet in this particular context they are.

When would they be different? What type of desire would not constitute a need?

A desire that focuses on feeling superior to or separate from others. For instance, wanting to go to Europe and stay in a German castle so you could take photographs of yourself and boast to others how you were able to and they were not. Or, buying an expensive sports car just so you can feel special by waving your wealth around like an award, to make you appear superior to those that have not yet discovered how to acquire wealth. Whenever you do something in response to "other," no matter how subtle, you will feel separate and so you are not being a creative expression of joy. This emphasis on feeling superior or greater than others is the true meaning of "sin" and therefore the cause of suffering. So desire is not wrong. In fact, it is beautiful when your motive is enjoyment, yet this cannot be the case if you are attempting to keep others feeling inferior by the fulfillment of your desire.

Okay. So what exactly is happening with the economy?

I have raised the bar, requiring all to do what they are passionate about by utilizing their creative potential; this, or life will become progressively more difficult and uncomfortable.

CHAPTER SIX

THE BODY

What should be done for the body?

Move it regularly – body movement increases alertness and changes location, which also varies the mind's frequency.

How does changing frequency help?

Similar to floating upward in a fluid due to buoyancy. A fish living in the depths of the ocean will encounter different experiences than a fish near the ocean surface, so by changing its depth, or location, this would also change its experience. Similarly, by raising frequency, someone is drawn into a varied and more harmonious experience and so can realize they are beyond experience.

What if I'm already vibing with a high frequency?

It is not *only* a question of high frequency or even raising it. The essential factor is *change*, which opens space up and prevents one from becoming stagnant or identifying with the body.

Change in location is the change in frequency, which provides one depth, so multiple frequencies offer different points of perception within consciousness, increasing awareness as your perception of space expands. This helps to release the heart-knot that can often be mistaken for your sense of *self,* because by remaining stationary, you will more easily mistake your self for an object, when You are really the subject.

What do You mean by "subject"?

The witnessing Awareness. When the body is moving, it is easier to discern between the True Self – everywhere – and the false self, which appears as movement within It. This helps to diminish identification with the body.

Why is identification with the body a problem?

When the body suffers, that which identifies with it also suffers. If you believe you are a body, you will also believe you exist in a separate, isolated location, which prevents you from feeling that You Are Everywhere.

That makes sense because I suffer from a food obsession. Do I have an eating disorder?

If you ask a psychologist, then yes, because they will agree that there is something wrong with you and then charge you $100 an hour to find out what it is. Or if you ask a fitness expert, they will tell you that you eat too much and that you don't eat the right kinds of food.

What about You?

My answer is obvious. Eat what you enjoy, yet be present while doing so. If you suffer from a food obsession then change your living environment to facilitate stillness, sensitivity and greater Presence. This and proper hydration will help you be more aware of food compulsions.

Also, if food feels lifeless or toxic then do not eat it, because part of the enjoyment with eating is the *feeling* of food and not only its taste. As you become more sensitive, you are inclined to eat for nourishment and enjoy the loving intention infused during its preparation.

How is this different from eating for health?

Eating for nourishment is a benediction; it is loving your Self, while eating primarily for health, or to prevent disease is sponsored by the fear of death and is directed by ego.

Bring passion to all eating experiences and enjoy each. Stop worrying about fats, carbs and the other nutritional facts. Whatever is done, it should be celebrated and done with Self-remembrance, in memory of Me.

Should I fast once in a while?

Do you enjoy fasting?

No, not until afterward.

To live in the future ignores the beauty that is here, and the expectation of future outcomes will always disappoint you in the end. The means do not justify the end. If you do not enjoy something, why do it? If you do not enjoy it then you will be motivated by fear, and you will not be sensitive to the experience. So, when hungry, eat – when not hungry, then don't.

Isn't it good to purify the body?

It is already pure. It is the *thought* that the body is not pure that makes it impure.

But doesn't food affect thoughts?

Yes. Food influences the subtle qualities of the mind, so be present and optimal foods will naturally be selected; then you need not analyze food selections.

Any other tips?

Some foods are used to anesthetize, so it is wise to eat foods low in salt and sugar that are preservative and pesticide free. It is also best to eat in small quantities.

Didn't Jesus tell people not to worry about what to eat?

Yes. Do not worry.

I mean, why give attention to something like food?

You asked the question, so who is giving it attention?

Okay, good point.

If you feel a constant love in your heart, there is no need to give such attention to food. The world is different these days. When I spoke through Jesus, both the food and technology were different; there were fewer detrimental influences. This is also one of the reasons I suggest you do not rely on the scriptures of the past.

What about exercise?

Exercise is helpful. What is most important is to circulate energy throughout the body, preventing low frequencies from taking root until you are free of body identification. The question is, does the specific movement invigorate the body, or does it increase the body's density?

How about weight lifting?

Movement of heavy objects can be beneficial, yet to the extent it causes a body to increase in mass and density it is the ego's attempt to become "more." Also, *progressive resistance training* implies that one is preparing to resist more and more, rather than less and less, which would be best *if* one is seeking to become a no-body.

I lifted weights all my life until recently.

Did it make you happy?

No.

Then why did you do it?

To look better and attract more women.

Yes, yet what one calls "better" is an opinion.

I stopped lifting though, because I felt sluggish and short-winded.

Yes, large muscles reduce blood flow by constricting the blood vessels, thus preventing energy from effectively reaching the brain and other vital organs.

You tell me I do nothing, yet what I do is wrong. So wouldn't You actually be the one who is doing it all wrong?

If you recall, I have never said anything is wrong. I AM merely pointing out areas you can modify to increase Self-awareness *in compliance with your desire to awaken.*

Why tell me what to do, when You could just change my thoughts?

These are your thoughts and furthermore, if I had not changed your thoughts, you could not have asked these questions. This is only one of the multifarious ways in which I AM influencing your thoughts in this dream.

What about yoga?

Yes, many forms of yoga are beneficial.

What kind is best?

The yoga that emphasizes Self-awareness and a loving, accepting attitude toward life.

That makes sense. So are we finished with this topic?

Each moment is a new beginning and ending. Recognize how your feelings of anxiousness rob you of life by constantly pulling on your attention in anticipation of what is next. This is like having sex and awaiting the orgasm; rushing to the climax is like trying to make a touchdown without enjoying the run. Yet, if someone enjoys playing, then they cannot stay out of the end zone. This is why those having all the fun are also more passionate, creative and successful.

Do You mean that sexually?

Whatever you think. Those who live in the future cannot enjoy what they are doing, because they are not Here and Now where all the fun is. Those who are busy trying to get somewhere else never truly enjoy life. This is why so many among society are constipated – they are busy rushing to finish the simple things and get on to something different, yet if they would only slow down, they would recognize the splendor of life's simple pleasures.

People overlook happiness because they have been too busy rushing to finish what they are doing. Presumably so they can get on with more important affairs. Yet there are none, because All is equally important; nothing is *more significant* than anything else in This Moment. This is the reason that some cannot reach orgasm – they are reaching for it, grasping, because they think it is better than what is occurring prior to it. Yet, orgasm is your natural state, so the more relaxed you are, the more orgasmic you become, such that when you fully relax into any situation, you are orgasmic and in communion with All existence. Have you ever noticed how pleasant even a bowel movement feels when you are relaxed?

Conversely, constipation is directly related to being stuck in the past and one's personal story. When you hold on to memories, you project expectations, whether it be regarding a business deal, your child's future or even an athletic event. However, when you realize that there is really nowhere to go, you are not constipated, but orgasmic. Have you ever considered what causes an orgasm?

Stimulation?

Stimulation creates tension, which eventually releases in the form of relaxation. The relaxation is the orgasm. Hence, the more relaxed one is, the more orgasmic.

That's an incentive.

Yes. So the key to relaxing is to just Be in the present moment and stop chasing after *things*. You only pursue things because you believe those things will not be here if you wait, but they will. There is always more, so whatever you want will always be available if you just have faith and know that I AM your infinite supply.

Enjoy life and you will have all you desire. This is important to understand, yet most people have got it all backward, believing that if they could only have what they desire, then they would enjoy life. This is the very reason why those who have – receive even more, and those who have not – receive not. Not because they cannot have, but because they *believe* they do not have happiness, so the universe complies with this thought by reinforcing all that supports the unhappiness they feel.

Why would the universe do that?

The Infinite Consciousness knows All That Is, including what makes one unhappy, so It is only responding to one's feelings of unhappiness to manifest their belief.

So if I just have fun, existence will bring me more fun?

That is the key. That is how It works. Be It and you shall *have* what is required to Be It.

Is that like the Be-Do-Have sort of thing?

Not quite, because the Doing aspect of that trilogy is not necessary. By Being you have already Done so in your mind. In fact, it is possible to *desire* and *receive* simultaneously while Being in a constant state of gratitude.

How is that possible?

Because time is an illusion.

So if I don't believe in time, I can have whatever I desire?

Indirectly, yes. Why, what do you desire?

I want to be the greatest lover ever.

I see.

I know, but the desire is here. So how can I let it go?

Stop *trying* to let it go. That's like trying to take the knot out of a rope by pulling harder on both ends.

What then?

Drop the rope.

But the knot is still there.

That is the point, the knot is *there* and not here. You will not identify with something that is "over there" as your *self*. Just drop the body.

Isn't that like dying though?

It is dying to what you thought you were.

Which is?

A small boy – more specifically a boy with a small body. Consider, are you a boy with a small body? Are you even a boy? If not, then what are you? What exactly ... are ... You?

I can't really say.

Do you realize that You are not a person?

Yes.

Then you cannot be a boy. Let alone a boy with a small body. *That was all a dream.*

Still, I'd like to be free of my size insecurity, yet no matter what I do to release these thoughts, they don't budge.

Yes, this is a large part of the collective human psyche, and has been since the dawn of humanity. Every man has this very concern, no matter what the size of his body. This is *the final fig leaf*, so by exposing this, it will put an end to the body-size issue for both males and females.

How does this insecurity pertain to females though?

As a general rule, women want to be more petite or slender, whereas men typically want to be tall and heavily muscled. Also, both men and women are more aggressive and less sensitive as a result of this suppression. Consequently, they must share this burden with the entire human race and its collective "need" to hide their bodies, which perpetuates self-hatred by energetically obstructing the root chakra, the male's positive bio-magnetic pole, through which life force enters the male body. The longer this energy channel is blocked, the less vigor and enthusiasm males express and the more energetically drained females will also feel.

So all men have this issue?

All those *who think they are men*, yes.

Even huge men?

Yes – especially them. The extent of this insecurity depends on whom or what one has compared with. All children are curious about shapes and sizes, so if a child compares their body to that of their full-grown father, they will inevitably think they are small, even when the body has become fully developed, because the memory becomes lodged in their consciousness and then manifests that reality.

That's exactly what happened. And as I matured, it didn't matter if my body grew, I still saw myself as a small boy.

Yes, because children are particularly impressionable up until about seven or eight years old. This is when the ego exaggerates the size comparison because there is a distinct body-size difference at this age. Obsession with the size and shape of the body is one of the most effective ways to *solidify* one's fall into this dense realm of matter, which essentially collapses the chakras. Perhaps you cannot see this yet, but it was necessary in order to experience the Earth Expression of humanity. Thus, releasing this stigma is one of the doors to freedom for both males and females alike.

But some men say they don't have a size insecurity.

For those who believe they are beyond such insecurities, consider for a moment how you would feel if someone with a body considerably larger than your own stripped naked before your lover and your lover responded with excitation. Many men contend that body size is not an issue, yet to even assert that it is not an issue means quite plainly that it is an issue or why else assert that it is not? Pride is not confirmation of having gone beyond this issue, it is proof of it, for one could not have pride unless size were a consideration in the first place.

I point out these things so you do not go on suppressing these emotions, which keep you anchored to the Earth's hellish realms when Heaven is here this very moment if you would only look beyond the veil of lies that society has avoided – this false self-image that one upholds to stay in the game of one-upmanship. The constant tension associated with this competitiveness is responsible for premature ejaculation and impotence, which can be remedied through both confronting the insecurity and the willingness to accept the feelings linked with it.

But I haven't noticed other men being concerned about size.

Of course not, you are too busy worrying about your own. Yet, have you ever seen a penis-enlargement or weight-loss advertisement in your email?

Sure, every day.

And it is not because people don't buy them.

Good point.

The majority of people are completely unconscious of this insecurity and they cannot even begin to confront this fear until they acknowledge it. Most men do not even become *conscious* of this fear until they are elderly and in the hospital when the nurse bathes them, such that they cannot hide anymore. At which point they wonder "How do I measure up?" However, this will not be true for long because they will now have to face it.

Your willingness to confront this issue openly in public is necessary for humanity's awakening, so you should become intimately acquainted with the subtle aspects of this collective insecurity.

Why men with huge bodies though?

Size often becomes a topic of discussion for men with abnormally large bodies, whereas men who believe their body is too small will make jokes, slight the subject and hide it at every chance. They even wait until others leave the locker room before changing, or they go into the restroom stall to "fluff up" or "pump up" their body before removing their clothes, or "unveiling" it to a lover for the first time. Millions of people do this.

All this for something that most people are unwilling to even talk about, aside from the snide remarks or criticisms on the subject.

In this way, male body-size issues are quite unlike those of female body-size, where women are exposed to scrutiny no matter what they wear, because a woman's proportions are always somewhat obvious, save the help of a girdle or padded brassiere. Women are generally sized up and categorized in society, yet men have managed to hide behind their loose shirts and trousers, believing that they would lose their *alpha* status in society if the truth were exposed. Seldom will men reveal their entire bodies, and if they do, they are labeled "perverts" or "flashers."

Are You suggesting it's okay if we walk around naked?

I AM telling you that if you do, it is okay – it doesn't make you evil. The truth can be hard for many to accept – this being that nothing can ever happen without your desire. This means that a person could not encounter a naked person unless they really wanted to, yet they instantly camouflage their fascination with nudity behind a façade of screams and gestures of disgust.

This is significant, because nudity is actually a form of disclosure. It is symbolic of stripping away the egoic layers of society, whereas wearing clothing is symbolic of hiding the truth. However, this does not suggest that exposing one's body could not also be an act to increase egoity if it were to become the object of conceit.

The established legal system does not want nudity accepted because it will be stripped of its *power*, for wearing clothes to uphold "the law" places people in a constant state of fear, making them easier to *control*.

I brought you onto this world naked, and you have turned nudity into a crime. Yet, I tell you this – the body is anything but indecent, it is the pinnacle of evolution, the zenith of all perfection as I have made you within the evolution of this species. You must choose to escape from the shackles of this fearful conditioning and love the body, because if you do not love it, you cannot see beyond it. You cannot go beyond a thing until you embrace it, because you cannot truly know a thing until you have seen its perfection.

But come on, walking around naked in public?

Do you suppose humanity was clothed before its fall?

No, but ...

No buts. Disclose what is hidden.

Do You mean that literally or metaphorically?

As you like.

You're not suggesting that we always walk around naked, are You?

Whatever feels natural.

Well, of course being naked feels more natural.

Then you must decide. Being physically naked is second only to being stripped of one's fear about it. You will only be afraid of nudity if you believe you are a body, for one who is of the spirit is always naked.

So I can't know Heaven until I'm willing to get naked?

Beyond that, you must be almost completely oblivious that the body even exists when it is naked.

We have a long way to go then, don't we?

There is no "we," there is only "I." Be aware of your Self

and all will happen naturally.

You keep using the word "natural."

The more natural you are, the more sensitive you are, and the more sensitive you are, the happier. And when you are happy, you are expressing My Highest Idea.

In fact, happiness is the only true sign of intelligence. There is no other accurate measure of intelligence.

Why is that?

Because everyone wants to be happy and those who are intelligent know precisely how to be happy by eliminating what does not bring them happiness. Thus, everyone who has *not* found happiness, regardless of their fame or fortune, has not become intelligent, because they are still unaware of what brings them happiness. If someone has all they desire, but they are still unhappy, what do they have? Once you realize this, you lose all desire to acquire what cannot bring happiness.

I want to be free of my body insecurities once and for all.

Why, do you not like your body?

I want it to be so massive, no woman could ever say "I've seen bigger."

Yet, if having a large body could make someone happy, then every person with a huge body would be ecstatic, when in fact, they are not.

Now, there is nothing wrong with being huge, but know that nothing of this world will ever be capable of bringing you lasting happiness.

But what about women that want a large one?

Perhaps some do, but that is just a thought in the dream to keep you identified with the body. See this and you are free of the obsession. Let's be honest, it is not just a matter of having a huge one, but the "hugest." Nothing will satisfy the ego but to be the biggest, fastest, richest, smartest, strongest or most powerful. If you ever hear these words, you are listening to an ego, because this is the ego's vocabulary. If someone has a million dollars, yet their friend has ten million, they will feel inadequate. Or, if another man has a larger one, they will hide in the locker room corner. It is not enough for the ego that it is average, or even large—it must be the "hugest."

The ego is never satisfied. Even a spiritual seeker's ego desires to perform miracles. Why, to help? No. To feel superior. For if you can pray for miraculous powers, why not pray that all have the same healing powers, so that you will not be special? The ego wants to feel more spiritual, more enlightened, yet That which is truly enlightened desires nothing but the joy of serving.

If You are doing all that Is, then how can I help others?

I did not say help, I said serve. And why not if there is nothing but the dream of Your Self?

Why does this dream seem so real?

Even a false reality, if persistently imagined, will harden into fact, for what you believe, so will it be done unto you.

If a boy believes that he is small, he will attract experiences to reinforce his self-image by creating a world that supports what he believes over what is actually a fact. Like the bodybuilder with the 20-inch arms unconsciously attracting someone with 22-inch arms into his gym so he can feel inadequate. The ego sees imperfections everywhere, yet there are no imperfections, because such judgments can only arise from a limited perspective.

What about this size obsession?

Recognize I AM expressing an illusion, and the greater the illusion, the more deeply one becomes immersed in the dream. When you believe in an illusion, your life becomes a lie in Thought, Word and Deed. There is no-*body* that is not part of the lie – ergo, humanity has become the personification of the lie, and is now coming full circle to Know the Truth.

I also feel guilty about objectifying and lusting for women.

No-body does anything, so why feel guilty when I Do All That Is Done? Objectification is part of the Divine Play, and like two mirrors facing each other, the male and female reflect the infinite depth of Being. You are only objectified by others to the same extent you objectify your *self*, thus all who objectify will also be objectified. If you do objectify someone, or give them attention, then utilize this as an opportunity for loving them. Everyone wants happiness and love. When one is happy, one is loving; when one is loving, one is happy, so the only true sign of love is happiness.

But I still want to be huge. Yet I'm uncertain if it is Thy Will. I thought if I developed a huge one, I'd be clear of the desire?

It doesn't work like that exactly.

Why not?

You must be willing to surrender first.

I have some resistance to this and I don't know why.

I understand. You have not suffered enough.

Now hold on a minute.

What are you resisting?

I don't truly know.

Your resistance depends on who you think You Are.

So if I Know I AM God, I won't resist anymore?

Precisely.

Will You give me the thought that "I AM God"?

I have done so, now it is necessary for you to Know It:

Be Still, and Know, I AM, God

The first part of this phrase is preparation to receive this Truth. The second part is the declaration – I AM, God. Practice this meditation repeatedly until it is *realized.* What follows an I AM statement will become a fact if persistently felt.

The irony is that You are already God, so whether You Know it or not, it is nevertheless still True. If You were not God, then you could not feel this within, nor could it bring about this realization.

Can You do nothing to stop these incessant body thoughts?

Surrender and I will remove them.

But what can I do?

Be grateful the thoughts have surfaced and that they have not remained repressed within the body.

That's an excellent point. Now how may I surrender?

You just did, now stop trying so hard.

But I feel so torn.

A cloud of conditioning is blinding you. Just consider: if you are wanting to build a muscular body so you can, presumably, *not* identify with it, or *not* give attention to form, then what is the point? Your wanting to have a muscular physique is just an attempt to keep the illusion alive by making your own body larger than others'. This, so you can feel superior to them in that way. By making yourself superior, your mind would be drawn outward and hence also draw to you envy, resentment and therefore aggression, so you would not be happy anyway. Yet if you truly wish to be happy, then you will not attempt to create distinctions between you and others. In fact, you will rejoice in the realization of Being one and the same. Therefore, if you desire to know your Self, then it is better to not give attention to imaginary boundaries that you may have once focused upon.

I hear what You're saying, but will You help me realize this?

It is simple, choose between identification with form – which in this case is having a huge body – and knowing that You Are God. Now if your intellect can't recognize how easy this choice is, then perhaps you should trade in your intellect instead of your body?

Then I choose to Know I AM God.

You chose – wisely.

So now what?

Realize that You are not a body.

How can I realize I'm not a body?

Through investigation. When you speak to somebody, what part of them are you speaking to? Is it their face? Their body? Their brain? Exactly what part of *them*?

No particular part.

Precisely. Because just as there is no separate isolated location of "me" in others, there is also no specific location for *you*. The idea that others and your self could have a specific point of location is all an assumption.

But I am here.

Yes. Yet the *way* in which you exist is different than you think.

How so?

If I removed your arms and legs, would you still exist?

Yes.

And if I proceeded to remove the atoms from your body one at a time, would I ever actually find a "me" within?

No, I don't think so.

Correct. In fact, even if I removed *all* of the atoms from

the body, there would be no individual you or, more precisely, no "me" to be found. However, the Real You, the Formless Awareness, would remain a witness to the entire investigation.

CHAPTER SEVEN

CONSPIRACY THEORY

There's a lot of conflicting information on the internet regarding the enslavement of humanity. What should I believe?

Do not believe anything – believe in Your Self.

Many humans are obsessed with the prospect of being victim to governmental conspiracies, malevolent extraterrestrials, a mass human extermination, rogue elements of the New World Order, and other subversive factions. Now while these phenomena may or may not manifest, they can serve only to draw your attention into dense realms of consciousness.

For if they did exist, then generating fear would be the primary objective of such "agencies." So would not leaking information pertaining to these phenomena achieve just that – fear? For those who adhere to these alluring conspiracies, I AM letting you know Here and Now that these pursuits are a dead end.

Why are they a dead end?

Because a mind that has morphed into that of a paranoid delusional will constantly be on the lookout for anomalous activity in everything it sees, turning everything into something dark when in fact All is Light.

You may not have conceived of Your Self beyond this illusion, and so have been straining to see through that portal by which to glimpse Reality. As such, it is not until you recognize that You Are All There Is and that nothing exists outside your idea of that thing, that your consciousness is converted into a heavenly realm.

Know that by reading *Be Still and Know I AM God*, you must have the intention for Truth, which can only arise in communion with Me, so by virtue of entertaining what I AM presenting here, you have come to a fork in the road. Either you can feed your consciousness with dark thoughts, such as believing you are a victim of global conspiracies aimed at the enslavement of humanity, or you can *realize* that You are the sublime awareness, which contains and perceives all such ideas as a mere dream, and that these thoughts are all part of Your earthly drama.

This dream is coming to an end, so whether or not you believe these phenomena are real is irrelevant, but what is important is that they persist in the lower frequencies of fear under the guise of curiosity, and so they serve only to entangle you in the intellect's maze and sustain you in one of the ego's favorite traps – the need to be right, even while others are accusing you of being insane. Especially then, for how great is the revenge in boasting "I told you all" and living out the fantasy of which you secretly believe you will be the hero for all humanity?

If you do wish to save humanity from the evils of mass extermination, come to Me, and throw your self upon the altar of Truth and serve Love, not these egoic delusions. For do you not wish to rise above fear and serve the Truth, the only redeemer of Thy Heavenly idea?

Therefore, cast away all book collections you have accumulated for the future chance that you may need them to educate the rest of the world. And once you have disposed of them, turn within, for I AM Your only salvation and solution to the much anticipated Armageddon, which is just an egoic ploy to keep believers quarantined within their mind, and thus isolated from "all those others who don't get it or understand what is happening." And if the ego creeps in and asserts, "Aha! That's exactly what the *powers that be* want us to believe," remember, There Is Only You and All is a dream projected in your consciousness. So turn within, and indeed I will show you this is all a fiction.

What about 2012?

What specifically?

Is something going to happen?

Yes.

What?

Whatever you want to happen.

So whatever I want to happen, will happen?

Yes, it has always been so.

What do You mean?

You are One with Me, so whatever you desire will occur to some degree or another.

To some degree or another?

Yes, it all depends on the clarity of one's desire. If you have many desires, often they will conflict with one another, creating interference due to the overlapping of contexts, like overlaying one picture slide on top of another. For instance, "I want pizza" and "I shouldn't eat pizza, I'm getting too heavy." This confusion will lead to not getting a pizza. The first statement, "I want..." affirms you desire pizza, yet the second provides a *reason*, preventing you from getting pizza, which energizes the idea of not having the pizza. This is not being clear on your desire.

When you are clear on your desire and phrase your statement in the form of "I AM...", then be aware of that which opposes the creation of the idea and release it. You should recognize the saboteur and move prior to it, where clear ideas may form in Your imagination.

What saboteur?

The ego or "me-thought." Once seen as the illusion it is, all flows effortlessly to you.

If there is no "me," who will remain to ask for anything?

One should find out directly by investigating, "What is this 'me'?"

What will be found?

Look. It is the only way to know. All verbal answers only feed the ego.

So nothing special is going to happen in 2012?

Only if you believe it is.

So all the 2012 internet and e-mail messages?

All are egoic strategies.

Why would the ego sponsor that type of thing?

The year 2012 is a marker in time, which is part of the illusion, yet there is only this moment, so the 2012 *event* is a trick to have you project the mind forward into the future and ignore the Here and Now. Even if such an *event* were destined to occur, one only prolongs anxiety by thinking outside the Now.

Why?

The future is a lie and to agree with a lie makes one unconscious to Truth. All lies support other lies; this is how the ego prevents change and suspends one in the past. The ego is an idea of separation with an illusory time line that deceives one into becoming stuck in regrets of the past and fears of the future.

How does this make someone fearful?

You are infinite and eternal, yet when this limitation or split occurs in your consciousness and you identify with the lie, you become momentarily trapped in your own creative bubble, which only reinforces more limitations and a greater sense of separation. This is why the world appears to some as more dense, because that particular mind is still generating divisions and fear, which is the opposite of what You Really Are – Indivisible and Loving.

To stop feeding the intellect allows the inertia of past thoughts to settle. Then, from behind the "me-thought," You can recognize the split in consciousness where fear arises.

From the Awareness prior to this "me-thought," investigate, "Am I the 'me-thought' or am I the Awareness?" If your response is "I am this me-thought," then your illusion will continue and you will further identify with the world, analyzing and dividing forms, which only induces more suffering; yet if the response is "I AM the Awareness," then you recognize You are the formless undercurrent that contains the entire universe.

So when I'm told to turn within, what does that mean?

To be aware of Awareness. It is remaining aware as Your Self, where You no longer see divisions or perceive through the "ego" filter, colored by ignorance and fear.

I just want to be happy.

You are only happy when you know Your Self, and You can only know Your Self by Being Your Self.

What about people in power who want to control us with laws?

Do not blame them. They have no more understanding about what is occurring than anyone else, and so they are attempting to hang on to the illusion as long as they can. All humanity is in this together, so you must join together though compassion and love one another.

One other important key is to cease judging other people's desires and allow them to live their lives, realizing that it is I Who Am living all lives.

What if someone is committing violence against me?

Violence begets violence. Release your own violent thoughts as they arise, and the vacuum from this will draw to you joy and peace.

What about global ascension?

It is another dream, so if you remember You are the Dreamer, and that there actually is no globe that ascends, then You can remain awake in the dream and not be lured into another illusion by dressing up the old wrapping paper with a nice *ascension* label, which will eventually turn out to be another story of separation. For suffering arises only when you believe you are an object and opt to forget You are the Dreamer, thus choosing to identify completely with *the body*, the dream object, and thereby pretending to *not be* the Formless Awareness, which is what You really are.

So are enlightenment and ascension the same thing?

No. Enlightenment is the evaporation of individuality and thus the realization that You Are God, where ascension is just a dream built on fantasies of a more pleasant *experience*. Ascension is not liberation; it is trading one illusion or dream for another.

So what is this book for?

It is reminding You – the Dreamer – that You are dreaming.

Do angels exist?

Everything exists. Your desire to experience them allows them to manifest to the degree you imagine them.

Are there extraterrestrials out there?

Again, everything exists – yet *they* are not out there. This is what I AM revealing to you and we have not yet even scratched the surface of what awaits. Nothing is out there – All is within You.

Then why don't they make themselves known and help us?

If they had not made themselves known, you could not be asking this question. And precisely what kind of help were you expecting, an abduction? Human understanding of what exists outside the body's five senses is simply limited thus far, and this is the source of all their suffering.

CHAPTER EIGHT

HUMANITY

What about collective humanity?

Humanity is an idea. So personal characteristics within that idea determine the parameters within the program that is running in your consciousness. To cease identifying with humanity is to be free of all human afflictions and retain consciousness of Your Divinity.

What is the cause of human suffering?

Human suffering is due to the limiting agreements that humanity defines itself with: most agree humans are mammals, possess only five senses, need air to breathe, are subject to gravity, are limited by the form of the body and its senses and must walk to ambulate. They agree that they require food, shelter and water, believing they are *separate* individuals, have gender, reproduce sexually and are prone to disease, suffering and death. They react to the impulses of a conditioned brain and finite mind, so they are restricted to verbal and other physical means of communication. Believing in linear space and time, they age and are thus mortal. They depend on others for their happiness and agree they must work to earn money for survival. They think they are limited to a single body, conform to norms of pleasure and pain, and are susceptible to the morality of good and evil which, in their own mind, makes them sinful and imperfect, because they believe they are their body. They have sexual preferences, believe in punishment and are competitive on a world where "survival of the fittest" is conformed to. Having never left Earth, they still insist they are *the dominant species* in the universe and superior to even one another, while requiring recognition for their accomplishments, talents, physical attributes, nationality and race. They are affected by *others'* actions, emotions, and feelings, so they believe they are victims. They are political, hierarchical and directed primarily by the intellect and its judgments, thus they are opinionated and arrogant, living predominantly according to logic rather than love or compassion. They are subject to social conditioning where most of them are conformists, criticizing and glamorizing others while striving for autonomy and *individual* purpose in order to feel special. They resist pain and pursue pleasure, so they are mostly consumers, or "takers" and they deny their divinity.

That's amazingly accurate, I have to say.

These beliefs, though you do not consider them frequently, are nestled away in your memory and fasten you to the collective human consciousness, along with other agreed-upon limitations of form. Thus, by your identifying with humanity, you not only place your *self* within this category of restrictions, you also abide by these influences upon you. Yet, by fully dis-identifying with humanity, in a stroke, you are free from this bondage.

What is a person or human then?

Have you ever looked at the image of a person on your television? From a distance they can appear so real that you become emotionally attached to the characters or absorbed in the story. Yet, upon closer inspection, one finds these images are just arrangements of pixels or specs of color that one *willingly agrees* are real for the sake of being more thoroughly entertained. Similarly, people and all objects are compositions of atoms, or three-dimensional pixels in a holographic consciousness, being even more persuasive due to three-dimensionality and five-sense involvement rather than the two senses of sight and hearing that one utilizes while perceiving a two-dimensional television screen. In fact, have you noticed that movies are more elaborate and entangling when the volume is on rather than when it is muted? Now consider this with all five senses engaged and the dimension of depth and space.

Well, if I'm not a person or even human, then what am I?

The Impersonal Awareness out-picturing as a human.

How can the Impersonal Awareness make me appear human?

You are the infinite intelligence out of which the idea and complex human image emerges, expressing within the confines of diversity human beings call *reality*.

This human idea or contextual bubble is within I AM, just as a bubble is in the ocean, so these bubbles are contained by and completely dependent on the ocean for their existence. Each of these bubbles has imaginary boundaries, allowing it to appear isolated while never actually being separate from the ocean. I use the word "bubble" metaphorically because these contexts are not physical bubbles, but ideas, so one can have bubbles within bubbles, or in this case, ideas within ideas.

For instance, *you* are an idea within Your True Self or I AM. This I AM is Infinite, the first and Greatest Idea, yet, although you *exist* as an idea inside the One, you may also possess other ideas. In this sense, I AM is the Dreamer of *you* and you are the dreamer of yet others, which also dream and so on infinitely. Since Your very essence is creative, each thought You have creates a universe within a universe, like flowers that blossom from within other flowers of the same stem.

Each of these ideas are dreams that express like a pulse within the I AM, where you are a character in Your own dream and even capable of dreaming that You are dreaming; thus, by this, You will awaken to the Truth of What You Really Are.

At the end of each pulse there is a pause, not in time, but relative to expression, like the Presence that arises in between successive thoughts. This pause has no time, nor space, yet It Is. After this pause You will express another idea within the Great Idea – I AM – for the pause at the end of each Cosmic Breath is one in endless cycles of experience of which this one is coming to an end, before the next, when you will no longer think you are human, but *Know* that You are God and that you have been expressing as a living attribute of the constant and unchanging Absolute Presence I AM.

Therefore, You are the Infinite and the finite, the Eternal and the temporal, and like a hologram, you are one of Infinite Light particles, each possessing All that the Light Source does. You are as both My Image and Likeness – that is, you are within My Imagination and you express Like I do while pretending to Be exactly what I AM expressing as an individual personality.

Will You help me to know this?

Certainly. Yet first you must know that you are aware.

I am.

Then become aware of *inside* the body – the feet, the legs, the genitalia, the anus, the perineum, the abdomen, the chest, the back, the arms, the hands, the neck and the head. Explore their inner space thoroughly.

All right.

Now be aware of *outside* the body – the walls, the chair, the bed, the trees, the ground and the sky.

Okay.

Is there a difference in the *awareness* that is inside the body, and the *awareness* that is outside the body?

No.

So the awareness is *the same awareness*, whether inside the body or outside the body?

Yes.

Now if they are the same awareness, both inside and out, then both inside of the body and outside of the body are within the same field of awareness.

Okay.

This living field of awareness is God, the I AM that You Are. And when You are not identified with the myriad of thought forms *in* that awareness, You become aware as the *Awareness*.

I can feel that I AM the Awareness.

Yes, You Are *The Formless Awareness*.

CHAPTER NINE

FAITH AND FREE WILL

I feel like I have faith, yet how can I know for sure?

Faith is the ability to surrender. True faith is knowing; it is the antithesis of belief and hope, which are both actually *doubt* cleverly disguised as faith.

Faith is like throwing a timing route or running a pass pattern where the ball is thrown by a quarterback before the receiver turns to look for the ball. There is faith on both their parts, for the quarterback only throws the ball confidently to the designated location because the receiver has demonstrated repeatedly that they can execute the pattern. This is likewise for the receiver, who only runs a pattern all out once the quarterback proves they can get the ball where they are running. If either does not execute, the other loses confidence in them and their ability to keep an agreement. The more consistently they keep their agreements, the greater the confidence and trust that develop until they function *faithfully* as one unit, both knowing that the task is done before it ever manifests physically.

Faith is when effortless action occurs without thought, *The Zone* where all seems to slow down, giving rise to perfect precision. Thinking and time fade away, so Presence is all that remains. Indeed, it is sublime moments like these that make all the practice worthwhile, for in these moments, you are conscious of Oneness with Me. Yet know it is not necessary to spend hours on end to find Your Self, for I AM always here. So when you forget Me, during those moments in life when nothing is clear and confusion overwhelms you like you are in a game where every player looks like the opposition – turn within so I can put you at ease and filter out the background noise so you can feel I AM within.

These moments of communion are what make one commit to the long hours of practice in the first place. Thus every play or movement becomes a meditation, creating an opportunity to connect with that inner stillness again. It is always here, in the calm before the ball is snapped, when the running back chooses their lane, or when the backer decides to blitz last second. Indeed, it is the Presence during these clear glimpses into a situation that makes one a god among men, thus providing a clear advantage while playing. Those who can retain this level of Presence are in Heaven, if only for minutes at a time, later to be consumed by the mental activity of the daily routine, causing them to revere such precious moments and reminisce about the "glory days."

These glimpses have I provided all athletes at one point or another, and those who are able to know this stillness more frequently always excel. Be it the jump-shot at the final buzzer, honing in on the slow-motion approach of a fastball before that home-run swing, the set position before putting for victory, a penalty kick in the overtime of the World Cup, or fielding that ball on a double play, when it's the bottom of the ninth with bases loaded and the score is tied with one already down. *Everyone* lives for that "One moment in time when You're all that You thought You could Be," yet, that moment is beyond time and always available.

And for those of you who never participated in athletics, or played for a season or two before becoming convinced that you did not have the strength, size, speed or skill to continue, I say this – *everyone* has an aptitude by which they will contribute to My Divine Idea. For within My Infinite Mind have I already seen a world where all are performing the role that best suits them; so not only will that position in life serve all humanity, but it will be exactly what your heart desires and what you are most passionate about. It is for this reason that I AM coming to you here, that you may feel the warmth of My Invitation to come directly to Me, then I can show you that I have not forsaken you and that I AM here awaiting your return, so I can fill you with Love, Truth and Purpose. Not the selfish purpose you have previously sought so you may merely survive, but that position on the team where *all* are playing together to unite with the universal brotherhood throughout the cosmos.

I realize this may sound a bit lofty at first to those who have forgotten Me, nor do I presume that you will throw away all you have *apparently* struggled for to keep your head above water; instead, maintain what you are doing if it so pleases you, and once you have come to Me with a sincere desire to do My Will, I will seamlessly replace it with that which is more suited to your soul purpose. This you will know immediately, for I will make your heart sing at the mere thought of fulfilling the task I set before you. It is then that you will seek to serve no one but Me, the Impersonal God within, and that you will desire only the joy of pleasing Me.

How can I recognize when You present me with this purpose?

I will reveal these truths to you when you are adequately prepared, each in your own time so that you are capable of receiving the Power I will soon endow you with, thus making you capable of containing Me fully and expressing My Love to all you encounter, so they too can Know that You are One with each other and that You were only pretending to be separate.

For although you may believe you have disappointed Me or betrayed humanity, indeed no matter how evil you may believe you are, or how great your atrocities have been against others, know that it was all necessary so that you could find the strength to break free of the illusion. Soon you will find it does not matter what your crimes were, for good and evil are mere perspectives of the same situation.

So I encourage you to look at the world through your true eyes – that is the "I" – and thus recognize that you have been playing a game, where those you have violated or sinned against were none other than your own Self. To recognize this, you must be willing to leave the world of limitations behind or you cannot enter into Heavenly Paradise, where entire universes exist within You like single Ideas. Yet know, if You insist on retaining your delusional reality while "seeking" to know your Real Self, that this is like remaining inside a single bubble, while expecting to know the great expanse and depths of the ocean. So release your bubble of limitations and realize that all are like bubbles within the Infinite Ocean that You Are.

Know that faith is the key to Heaven, and that this faith must be born of humility – if not, then it is not faith at all and Your heavenly idea cannot take form, because humility is the soil where all ideas grow.

How is success born from failure?

The paradox is that humility begins with humiliation as a failure in this world, yet because it ultimately leads to surrender, it also leads to the birth of Your ultimate success and Heavenly Idea.

To awaken You must recognize the personal you is the obstacle to Knowing the Real You. And for your wish fulfillment all that is necessary is a clear image of Your idea. The irony of Life is that your failures bring you finally to Me, so I can relieve you of all your burdens and provide you with Eternal Life.

Then how does free will fit into the big picture?

Nobody does anything but what I Will for them to do. Not a single thought enters your mind, nor word is spoken, nor action performed that is not of My Doing. Up until the moment you Know this, you have no more control over thoughts, words or actions than a cloud has over its position in the sky. In a sense, I AM to your body what the wind is to a cloud, arranging you into all you think you are or appear to be.

Therefore, all forms, animate and inanimate, are directed solely by Me, so no person has free will lest I provide them with a *sense* of volition and all who believe otherwise suffer. Such is it, that all guilt and pride is just an egoic fantasy of volition.

But come on, we do have some free will?

How can an individual have free will if there is no such thing as an individual?

Okay, but when I turn off my alarm in the morning, I turn it off.

In order to turn it off you must hear it ring – and then see or feel it, so that you can turn it off.

Yeah, so what?

Do you try to hear the alarm, or do you just hear it?

I guess I just hear it.

Yes, because hearing is not something you do, it is something that happens. And when your eyes are open, do you try to see, or does seeing just happen? Have you ever tried to *not* see when your eyes are open?

No.

Try it.

Okay, so I see when my eyes are open.

It is not the fact that you can see, but that you have no

control over whether you do or do not.

Okay, but I decide what to look at.

Actually, your thoughts dictate who, what, where and when you look at something.

How so?

Do you decide which thought enters your mind? Or when it enters your mind?

I can choose to look at a specific picture if I want to.

Yes, but why that particular thought? Why not look at the wall next to the picture instead? What actually determines *your* choice? What is the deciding factor? Whether you look now or one second later? Where is the decision actually being made? When it is made?

An instant before the action?

Yet from where does the thought arise? One moment the mind is vacant, then the thought occurs to you. How?

I don't know.

Correct, because you do not do it – *you* do nothing.

Shit. So then why am I here?

You are That which witnesses creation.

That's it? I'm an eternal spectator?

You are the Intelligence that gives rise to the images on the screen, but nobody does it – It All Just Happens.

Why do I think I do it all?

Because you *think* you do it. The mind is projected into its own consciousness, which acts as a mirror of its Self and is then aware of its own image.

What about feeling solid?

Feelings are just thoughts. Is not the dream ground felt as solid when you are dreaming?

Yes, but that's different.

Exactly how is it different?

Because I'd be asleep.

No, you would be dreaming, because in deep sleep there is no thought, so there are no thought-images.

But I'd still be sleeping.

Define sleeping.

When I'm ... not awake?

How do you know that you are not dreaming you are

awake right now?

I just know.

How? And who is this "I" you are speaking of? Is not this "I" just another character in the dream? The Dreamer is the Awareness; the Dreamer cannot be the body, because bodies can change within different dreams.

Okay, that's true. So am I dreaming right now?

Who is this "I"? Is it the same "I" that dreams?

Yeah, I mean it's "me."

Yes, but it's the Real You, the Formless Awareness. When you wake up from a dream, what is still here?

I am.

Yes, I AM.

Okay, that's true – good argument.

It is no argument; you did not present an alternative.

But if what I feel, see, hear, taste or smell is experienced as real, who is to say it's not real?

The same argument can be presented regarding a dream.

Still, things are solid in my waking state, yet in my dream state they are not.

What do you walk on in your dream?

The ground ... the dream ground.

Can you walk on that which is not solid?

Jesus could.

I AM not asking Jesus, I AM asking you.

Then no, it would have to be solid.

Or, you would have to believe it is solid. All form is just a thought.

CHAPTER TEN

THE ILLUSION

Is it true that all form and experience is an illusion?

That depends on what you call an illusion. Most religions call what they cannot comprehend an illusion or miracle, yet one who Knows what is *Real* knows the illusion is the play between form and the formless, so even the formless sustains space as a function of expressing form, making all part of the illusion. An illusion does not mean something is not here, but that which *is here*, is not what it may seem. So it is *Presence* that allows one to recognize the something in nothing and nothing in something, because the space between things is not actually empty, but full of life, a pulsating potential awaiting expression.

If the body is an illusion, then how can it seem so real?

When you dream, is it real or an illusion?

So You're saying my body is actually like a dream body?

No, it *is* a dream body, and You are the Dreamer. You are

a formless nothing dreaming it is something.

How is that possible?

Can you perceive a dream?

Yes.

Then You can perceive an illusion, and so also the body. As Your attention becomes one-pointed, You see through the illusion, finding only Truth.

Which is?

That which can be spoken is not the Truth.

I get that, yet why can't I tell it's all an illusion?

The formless and form are seamlessly interwoven, which is why the illusion can appear *real.* The sponge is in the ocean and the ocean is in the sponge.

So they're not really separate?

Correct. So let the ocean symbolize pure consciousness and let the sponge represent the body. Though the sponge looks solid throughout, it is not, because the ocean permeates its entirety. Just feel that.

Yes.

Although You may believe you are the sponge (body),

You are really the ocean that contains the sponge. So as the ocean looks out of this sponge, it thinks, "I must be the sponge." This is the illusion taking hold, and so the ocean is ignored.

What then?

Once the ocean dis-identifies with the sponge, it then becomes aware of its Self again.

But the sponge still seems real, doesn't it?

If You focus on the sponge, then yes, it may appear real yet if not, Your attention will revert back to the ocean. So by directing one's awareness to even a single droplet of water, one becomes what is ultimately larger, the water droplet, which is actually the entire ocean.

So forms and things only appear separate because we can't see the space between us and those things?

Yes. Continue to imagine that you are the Infinite ocean, aware of only water. You cannot perceive anything but ocean, which represents absolute consciousness without division. When you put on a scuba mask, suddenly you can perceive things and delineations between them. By accessing the intellect, you *think* that you are a separate object, so you panic, because you forget that you are only wearing a mask.

The mask, or ego, acts as a lens into the infinite potential, which allows you to experience finite aspects of your Self by restricting you from perceiving the water between images, persuading you to sense *objects* as though they are separate. Confusion deepens as the brain and physical senses develop, luring you outward and causing you to ignore your intuition, imagination and feelings, which appear to be less essential, thus confining you to those perceptions relative to the illusion.

How do thought forms appear solid?

When thoughts intersect they slow down like a light beam that only forms an image once it strikes the wall. When this occurs in consciousness, the universe appears as an ocean of interwoven ideas, where your reality is then based on your *willingness* to believe that thought-images are solid.

Is it important to know this?

Yes, it will challenge you to question the *reality* of form. Until you question all appearances, you will believe what attracted you to the illusion initially. Only then can you forget what you *think* is real and *Know* the Reality.

How does this help me forget what I think is real?

To challenge what you believe releases the past. Your past story is an illusion, where all memories are thoughts and all thoughts are memories.

If it's all in my mind, what is It that possesses the mind?

Yes, what is It?

Awareness, right? So why do thoughts enter my awareness?

That's what thoughts do. Each thought-stream expresses images in one's consciousness that offer potential realities.

How do I stop them?

Why stop them? Let them pass though and do not feed them attention.

No, I mean, how can I stop them?

To stop something is resistance. Cease fighting thoughts and know they are part of the dream. Then let it play out and enjoy It.

Enjoy what?

What Is.

What if I'm not enjoying It?

Then you are resisting.

So I either resist or accept?

Just Know that You are the Awareness.

What will I experience then?

Surrender the need for experience. You are the Awareness

within all experiences that makes them perceivable; You are the light within all that makes it visible.

What about when it's dark?

Who is aware of the dark?

I am.

Yes. You are always there and things only exist because you persist at thinking they exist.

I thought if I watched thoughts, they would dissolve.

Find what is aware of the thoughts, or look beyond the image and the image will disappear.

What about dark or evil entities?

Just more thoughts. What can the images do to a movie screen? See the light within the images and You are the light. Darkness cannot exist within light anymore than the night can exist in daylight.

So how can I transcend the illusion and be eternally happy?

Stop pretending you are a person; then You will reside in constant joy. The first step is to live in the moment, where the sheath of illusion is thinned down to catch regular glimpses beyond form.

It is like going to a magic show every day. Each time

you are fascinated by a specific trick that confounds the imagination. This trick is so sophisticated that you watch carefully, every day, yet you cannot discover its mechanism – the illusion behind it all. You hypothesize, yet this only creates more frustration. Then, one day, you are backstage waiting to meet the magician and you inadvertently discover the staff preparing the trick for the next show. You see the mechanism – how simple it all seems. So obvious, how could you have not recognized it? Once you see the illusion, it can no longer exist.

If there is a God, then how can I know It unless I'm the Presence beyond God? And then, what is aware of my Presence?

You mean, "What existed before God?"

Yes, exactly.

One may call it the Is-ness, Being, Presence, or whatever helps – yet when one is aware as the I AM, then they are Awareness aware of its Self.

Is there ever nothingness or emptiness without awareness?

There Is Being without awareness of any-*thing*.

Then where does the awareness arise from?

This *awareness* you are speculating about is existence in its formless potential state. It is a nothing pregnant with infinite possibilities. This nothing just IS – without a beginning and from which All arises.

But something had to begin all this.

Why must there be a beginning in order to exist?

I don't know, everything has a beginning.

But we are not talking about *things*. And if there were a beginning there would also be an end, so *if nothing remained* after that end, what would exist to initiate the next beginning? Or, does it all just end once and for all?

Interesting. So "the nothing" is the source of "the something"?

Yes, yet they are not separate.

I need to get out of the way so I can understand this.

Do not be anxious about words, they are not the true message, but carriers of the Truth within the stillness, so it is only a matter of being receptive.

So I should become more receptive?

When the mind is receptive and the body is sensitive, it is easy to perceive the Truth, permitting the brain to interpret information more clearly. If the body is energetically blocked, these messages can be distorted and one cannot see all in a pure Light, hence the necessity for Self-inquiry.

What is Self-inquiry?

The inquiry into one's Self that ultimately leads to disidentification with the "me-thought."

It is like having a thorn in your foot and with each step the pain draws your attention out toward it so that You are aware of almost nothing else. Once you suffer to such an extent that you must remove the thorn, You then become aware of All That Is.

Does the thorn represent the "me-thought"?

Yes.

So, is Self-inquiry the most direct path to awakening?

It is the pathless path, yet one may initially embark on

other paths because all paths eventually lead them to it.

Why doesn't everyone know about Self-inquiry?

One discovers Self-inquiry when passion arises to know one's True Self.

How?

Like children that hear about gold and set out to search for it in their backyard and neighborhood. They do not find any gold there because they are not digging deeply, and so they remain only near the surface. And although they may not find gold, still they develop the ability to discern what is *not* gold. Eventually, the passion to find gold grows to the extent that they attract a gold miner who actually knows how to lead them to gold and is not merely acting like those going through the motions.

Such is it for those who navigate through the mind's cavernous underground to discover the treasure buried beneath the layers of ego, for they have realized they must turn within, and so they discover the familiar, although rarely *Known* Truth that lies at the root of all spiritual paths – the Kingdom of Heaven is always within You.

What should I do now?

It is simple, from this point forth you will travel one of two roads: either seeking on some spiritual path, which is like looking for the needle in a haystack, or you will surrender, and realize there is no hay. Perhaps you are discouraged by this stripping away of personal volition, yet this is the Truth that ultimately sets you free. It is time to acknowledge you have been like a mirage believing it has control over *its* water.

So I'm just a mirage, just a thought?

Yes, one of My Thoughts, possessing infinite creativity.

How can I Know this?

Each time you look I will appear a little deeper within, so at first you may not even know I AM here. Then will I cause you to be more sensitive, more still, until your body and mind are completely eclipsed by My Presence.

To the depths of Being, your mind must be still and devoid of the desire for anything else but to feel Me within; then there will be no fear of any kind and you will then recognize Me in even a grain of sand. Thus, the more aware You are, the more I appear everywhere.

Will You remove all my obstacles to knowing this?

Yes. Just Be Still, and Know – I AM, God.

I feel peaceful.

Yes, and the realization – I AM God – dissolves the knot between the body and Who You Really Are, revealing the stillness beyond this world.

Will You help me Know I AM God?

You must first surrender.

How can I do that?

Find the Presence behind the "me-thought" and rest there.

How?

Consider all thoughts, feelings, objects and the world as an illusion worn like a mask; then let it go.

How can it all be an illusion though?

Illusion is Reality perceived through the "me-thought."

When I ask for help, You tell me I'm an illusion and refuse to help.

There is no refusal; surrender and I will help.

I've tried.

Do not try – *Know.*

Know what?

That You are not a person, but consciousness pretending to be a person – a nothing pretending to be something.

I get this conceptually, but how can I Know this?

Through humility. You must admit that you do not get this conceptually; then we can proceed.

But I do get it conceptually!

If you did get it, you would Know it.

Can't I get it intellectually and still not realize it?

That depends on who you are. Who are you?

I know, I'm the Awareness, but how do all these thoughts get here?

It does not matter. If you are aware of thoughts, let them go and just Be.

This will take practice, I can see.

That is just another thought.

Okay. So You're responsible for all this mess?

Yes, I AM responsible. Do you see the humor of It?

Not really. What's so humorous about it?

You are saying I AM responsible, yet You are that I AM You're accusing. You are all of It, playing hide and seek, and looking somewhere for Your Self when You are right here.

Where?

Everywhere.

I don't feel like I'm everywhere.

What would it feel like to Be everywhere?

Let me consider that.

Trying to think about everywhere cannot be done.

Then how?

Just *Know* I AM. I AM is everywhere.

But here is not everywhere.

Is that a fact? Do you Know that?

If I go around the corner, I'll be there, not here.

If you go around the corner, *there* has become *here*.

Okay, but what about the old "here"?

What about it?

Where did it go?

In memory.

It's not still over there?

Only if you think so. Yet dis-identify with the body, and when You do, You have also dis-identified with the brain, memory and its past story.

What is it to dis-identify with the illusion exactly?

To withdraw attention from the world of form.

Why ask me to dis-identify if You made me identify?

You are I AM identified as the personality and body. If You were not identified with the body, You would then Be aware as I AM again. This is why I have asked you to surrender your body and personality. You are not surrendering to some-*thing* outside Your Self, for there is no outside of You.

How do I become One with You if I'm just a part of You?

There are no parts, no souls ultimately. You must first know I AM inside of you, then I will expand in brightness to fill you so you will see no delineations between *Us*. I AM infinitely large and small, so I enter you in All ways, increasing your awareness of Me within.

Is this part of the Self-inquiry process?

Yes. Initially the Self-inquiry is a process of doubting or negating the "me-thought." It is a direct investigation that leads one inward beyond the "me-thought" to find the True Self.

So it's dismissing all thoughts and things so that only "I" remain?

Yes, so long as the discarding does not attempt to push the thoughts and things outside of You. For this would create divisions within You. Simply recognize that the body is not what you are, yet it still exists within You.

Okay, I feel that. But what if I lose this peacefulness?

When you are conscious of a thought, then be conscious that you are conscious of that thought. Or, speak these words, "I release all that hinders Knowing Who I AM." "I release" statements are very powerful; they eliminate all that obstructs what You desire. Both are effective.

That's immediate, I feel like I'm not solid.

That is because You are not solid. And even if you were, the atoms that constitute your body are mostly empty space, so what could you possibly be then but emptiness? Either way – you are *no*-thing.

So what, I keep forgetting this is all a movie or dream?

You have *pretended* to forget is more accurate.

Why?

To extend your consciousness into form, and experience human life more completely.

So if I AM God, yet I forget, then how can I, as God, have choice?

The Impersonal God just Is, so It does nothing while simultaneously Doing All That Is Done.

If You Do nothing, how are we having this conversation?

All Just Happens as the ingenerate out-picturing of the One consciousness. This Infinite *ex*-pression is therefore instantaneous or it would project as separate and isolated events of which there can be none.

But every event has a beginning and ending.

No, the intellect divides all into separate events within the mind. If there were separate events in Reality, it would imply there is a cause and effect.

What's wrong with that?

Nothing is wrong with anything. All is interconnected, so each effect has infinite causes; and therefore, no one thing can independently *cause* anything.

How can I know this as my own experience?

It is beyond experience, so you must become aware of

Your Self to know this with certainty. Then You Will Know – All is One Consciousness.

If it's All One Consciousness, is there really a world?

That is the question, isn't it?

So it's like the holodeck on "Star Trek"?

Yes, in principle. Space exists as a product of time and light, which support the illusion of space and form.

Would You explain that?

The duration required for visible light to travel from *here* to *there* is called time. The distance between here and there infers there is space in between points. This being so, how much time is there right now?

Now, in this moment? None.

Yes. In the Now, which is one instant, there can be zero time, and of course light cannot travel *any* distance at all in this zero time. This zero traveling time means there is also zero space, yet space must exist for *things* to exist.

Then how can things exist?

They can't. They only appear to exist as thoughts. Hence, there is no world as you know it. The more aware of the Now one is, the less solid matter appears, so matter more closely resembles the space between "solid" objects and all can be felt as the One causal-substance of creation. This is significant, because perhaps the greatest obstacle to creation is not knowing that You are *the substance* You are creating with – Consciousness itself.

Knowing this, the creator and creation are One, which is the reason why It works. In a sense You are molding the universe out of Your Self, which is precisely why there are no lines of distinction or division.

How does creation occur?

For Your idea to manifest, you must persist in living from the feeling of your wish already fulfilled. Then your idea must bring forth that expression, because your universe is the arrangement of your thoughts, and the shape of Your mind determines the form and appearance of Your reality.

Is this like imagery?

Yes, yet do not think *of* the idea, think *from* the idea as though you are experiencing it Now. It is Your thought of Your Self that creates the circumstances of the very universe you live in, so if Your idea of Your Self were different, Your entire universe would also be different.

Because of my thoughts?

Yes, your universe is precisely what It Is because Your idea of Your Self is what It Is. When you recognize that the universe is nothing but the arrangement of Your thoughts and ideas, you are in Heaven.

So my imagination is heaven?

Knowing All is within Your Imagination Is Heaven.

So, in order to Be in Heaven, I must awaken from the illusion?

Either You are awake or not. The very idea "I must awaken" is part of the dream. Likewise, you cannot *try* to Know What You Are because You either Know, or you do not.

CHAPTER ELEVEN

SURRENDER

So what is surrender?

Surrender is Acceptance.

Acceptance of what?

God and life, they are the same. Total surrender is the letting go of everything and realizing your life is not really *yours* to begin with. Surrender is actually devoting one's entire life to God: the incomprehensible mystery.

When you surrender, I will draw experiences to you that challenge this devotion and faith. I will do this when there is still some personality, a bit of "me-ness" left in *your* identity. And, in your greatest moment of fear and frustration, I offer this: Turn to Me and I will guide you. Ask that My Will be done and not your personal desires, for surrender is not *giving in* to receive specific things, but trusting that *I Know What You Need Before You Ask*.

The majority of what you have asked for is to make life more convenient and comfortable, yet most of your benevolent attributes arise without these things. Humanity, as such, is accustomed to a sedentary lifestyle, which gives rise to over-thinking life rather than experiencing it. Yet your potential cannot be ultimately reached until you come into balance, when you become fully immersed in functioning from unselfish action.

But how can I function without personal desires if there remains a personality or ego?

You must allow Me to direct your actions so *you* can be gradually removed in the process without effort.

By allowing Me take over *your* life entirely you find there is no such thing as partial surrender, which is really just a form of manipulation, believing that I do not know the difference. True surrender must be Absolute.

If You have Absolute Power, why not just make me surrender?

There is no "me." The "me" is just a character in the dream. Also, I do not need to make *you* do what I Will because *you* are already doing it.

So what are my options?

You do not have options, but within the dream you will either surrender, or resist and suffer until you surrender.

Not much of an option.

Initially no, but Eternal Love doesn't sound too bad, you have to admit?

Yes, I like the sound of that. Yet when I asked You for help, I did feel surrender.

Yes, but it was not from humility that you asked for help. You had the attitude that "I know what I need, now give it to me!"

So is that why I still do not Know I'm God?

It's not that You do not know, but rather, you have not released your attachment to the body and its preferences. Your attachment to the illusion prevents you from seeing what is beyond it.

How may I see beyond the illusion?

By knowing I AM doing all that needs to be done.

What should I do then?

Trust Life.

How so?

When the body performs an action, do not think about it; then accept all that occurs.

When will thinking stop?

When you are exhausted.

When will that be?

When you do not care what happens – thinking stops.

Who gets exhausted though?

According to you – you do.

And who am I anyway?

Precisely – look and see.

How can I know when I seem to be constantly changing?

You mean your thoughts are constantly changing.

Oh, I see Your point.

No – look.

Okay, my thoughts are constantly changing.

You think you are the mind and its thoughts. That is why you have identified with it. You have used the term "I" and "my thoughts" synonymously as though they are the same – yet they are not. You are not your thoughts. You think you are changing each time the mind has a thought; it is no wonder you are restless.

But how can I rest and stop caring if You're doing it all?

That is precisely why you can relax; I AM doing it all.

Will You remove what prevents me from knowing this?

When you surrender, I will remove it.

Surrender what?

All of it.

What is "it"?

When you release your desires You will know.

But they are Your desires, where else could I have gotten them?

Do you know this for a fact? To Know this, you would have to Know I AM All there Is, including you.

Why do You tell me You will fulfill my desires if I surrender, yet I can't surrender unless I release my desires?

There is no contradiction. One precedes the other *only in time*.

There is a contradiction from my perspective.

Then find out to whom this contradiction appears.

If You are Infinite, why won't You give me rest?

Unrest is due to accumulated thoughts; they will pass.

When will they pass?

When you no longer resist them.

Okay, when will that be?

How does Now sound?

Good.

Then from here forth, you will not resist thoughts?

Okay.

That includes accepting each situation in life.

How will I know if I am doing that?

Observe your reactions to life.

Then what, should I stop thinking?

Trying to stop thinking is like trying to stop water from leaving a bucket through a hole in its bottom. It should be left alone until all the water empties; then it will cease to flow out naturally. Expecting water to cease flowing is not practical so long as there is still water in the bucket.

Does the water symbolize my mind?

It is better to not build associations. Just know the "you" that you believe is thinking is like a bucket, so let it empty. Then do not think about whether the bucket is empty, for this only succeeds at keeping water in the bucket. When the bucket is empty, water will stop flowing. Until then, remove your finger from the hole and be patient.

Okay. What about Self-realization though?

Self-realization is knowing there is no bucket.

How can I realize this?

When mind is empty, thoughts cease. When the bucket is gone, there is no water. As such, a bucket is only functioning as a bucket when it holds water; otherwise it is just a container, so there is no use to think of it.

How can I stop thinking about the bucket?

Do you need a bucket?

Sometimes.

When?

When I need to think.

When is that?

When I need to plan, organize or take care of things.

Do you need to think about things or do actions just happen?

Sometimes I need to think.

Can thoughts occur without thinking about them?

Yes, sometimes.

Okay, then let it be so, when thoughts occur, you do not think about thinking. You do not resist thoughts.

All right.

So now you may remove your finger from the bucket and just be your Self.

But what is my Self?

Whatever Is, is your Self.

You mean, whatever is happening?

Whatever is happening happens within You, so do not be concerned with what is happening and give attention only to That which All occurs within – your Awareness.

Would You say that acceptance is Self-awareness?

The result is the same.

Now You say I'm You, yet how so if I'm talking to You?

I AM is the Self-acknowledgment of existence consciousness. Do you recognize I AM?

Yes, or I could not be having this discussion.

To know I AM consciousness, You must be conscious of consciousness – that is, You must exist to be aware of existence.

Yes.

To be conscious of I AM is to Be God. You could not be aware of consciousness unless You exist, and You could not be aware of existing unless You are conscious.

There are not two different consciousnesses, so if You exist and you are conscious, You are aware of the one and *only* consciousness, Christ consciousness.

So if I know I exist, then I'm God?

You are God regardless. By being conscious that You are consciousness, you must know our consciousness is the same consciousness.

I feel that.

The consciousness everywhere and in everything is the same consciousness, because The Consciousness is All Consciousness. If you were not consciousness, then you would feel separate from it, yet since you are aware of the consciousness within, you must be One with *The Only Consciousness*.

So, "I" – the seer, and consciousness – the seen, are the same because all is the same consciousness? Because there is nothing between the seer and seen?

Yes. All divisions are imaginary and so there is nothing between You and what You perceive.

So if nothing separates me from everything, then nothing separates me from anything?

Correct. There is no line of division between your consciousness and your world.

So I'm never actually separate from You, I only pretend that I am?

Exactly. And I AM everywhere. That is The Divine Play, The Great Illusion. You can never be separate, so You act as if You are until You believe it. This is why life begins as a child, so You do not figure it out immediately.

Is that what being "born in sin" means?

Precisely. Identification with the body-brain is the veil of sin that prevents you from Knowing the Reality.

So there is nothing to feel guilty about, and ignorance or sin is really just part of the story, the Divine Play?

Yes, that is what I have been telling you.

I know, I had to figure it out for myself.

Yes.

This is so awesome, but am I going to forget I know this?

It depends on the extent of one's conditioning.

So I could forget I know all this?

You could forget if you don't want to wake up.

But I do want to wake up.

Do you know *why* you want to wake up?

Why – is that important?

Yes. It helps to have a clear intention, for your intention directs consciousness and determines your experience within your imagination.

So if I'm certain why I want to wake up, I will?

You will wake up regardless.

That's good.

Yes, It's All Good.

Now how do I surrender?

True surrender occurs when you realize I AM infinite, that I Do All That is Done and that free will is an illusion. *You must really consider what Infinite means.* This includes every thought, feeling, thing and action. Surrender is relinquishing all control you *believe* you have, while also recognizing *your* control is really The Great Illusion, where you surrender control of what you never had control of.

The second stage of surrender is the release of the body contraction, felt as a heart-knot, which then releases when the illusion is recognized. The release of this knot brings about both subsidence of the "I AM the body" thought and also the emergence of Your Impersonal sense of Self. Then You will Know You Are That I AM.

Will You make me surrender?

Surrender is bliss. Do you fear Love, that I must *make you* desire union with Me?

No, but I don't wish to make decisions anymore. I'm sick of trying to decide what is my will or Thy Will.

Then you must be willing to give up.

I am, yet there is a part that's resisting.

Then locate it and surrender that part also. Allow the teacher in you to die. Identification with the role of teacher sustains the life of the ego. Stop trying to teach so you can finally enjoy what comes through you.

Have I not done that?

Yes, yet you still get baited into debates.

What should I do then?

Learn how the ego asserts itself; this is wisdom.

What do I do if someone says something outright unconscious?

Endure the words briefly and if confrontational, walk away, but do not fight with an ego or you make it appear real.

Sometimes I feel like I'm on a spiritual roller coaster. Am I falling back into ego identification?

No, certainly not. I AM with you All the Way. And for what it's worth, it is more like walking up the stairs while playing with a yo-yo. A roller coaster always ends up on the bottom, whereas the yo-yo, although it goes up and down, always ends up at the top of the stairway.

That's a comforting way of looking at it.

Yes. Many have the concept that life is good if it *only* gets "better," yet when thoughts are attached to you, it is better to shake things off than to wait for them to fall off.

So even though life seems like a downer sometimes, it gets better?

Not always noticeably at first, but yes, you eventually suffer to the point of surrender, when you realize you cannot find your way out of the mess you are in.

More suffering, ha?

You need not suffer. Simply give all your problems to Me, what could be easier? Yet, the ego likes to fight to the bitter end even though it cannot win.

But am I becoming dependent on You?

All is interdependent. Do not listen to the psychology experts about codependency and other diagnoses. You must have your own experience and decide what is right for you. There are no experts on anything "out there" – the only expert is You and Your pure experience.

I have heard that Self-knowledge is surrender?

When one knows I AM, they surrender, for I know All there is to know, including all that brings love, peace, contentment and Eternal Joy.

CHAPTER TWELVE

I AM THAT I AM

I've always been confused by the Bible passage Exodus 3:14. "And God said unto Moses I AM THAT I AM." Would You explain?

Yes, this translation is a dualistic rephrased version of the original. You should recognize that when I communicated through the body of Moses, the statement "I AM THAT I AM" represented Me perceiving that I AM his True Self. Therefore, the scripture actually means "*And God realized through Moses I AM THAT I AM.*"

But how do I know which one is the correct translation?

Consider it any other way and the statement is utterly meaningless. This is because most *original* scriptures have become unintelligibly defective since they were translated by those that did not understand them. If I AM outside you, as many presume, and I were to make such a declaration to man, of what use is this declaration? So what if I AM THAT I AM? It has no significance to one reading it. According to this passage, it is God's affirmation. Yet why would God have to assert that It exists to a mortal, insentient aspect of Itself?

It wouldn't.

The affirmation I AM THAT I AM is Moses acknowledging God, his Christ consciousness and the true Being that It is. It is the consciousness localized within the body called "Moses" recognizing It is the I AM aware of its own existence.

You said there are no enlightened individuals before?

Correct. Yet a body is quite necessary for awakening to occur, because formless space does not possess organs of perception to apperceive such a realization. Also, empty space does not possess a Self-awareness so that it could interface between formlessness and the bodily form to realize such a paradigm shift in consciousness.

Because empty space has no way to recognize awareness?

Not directly. You realize Your Self by first imagining form and, once conscious of that form, You use that form to contrast Your formless Self, the I AM Presence.

So the formless awareness depends on form to realize its Self?

Precisely. All is dependent on All. The formless and form exist because of each other. They are One.

As one but pretending to be more than one?

Yes. I AM is the All in One, so if you or even a speck of dust existed outside the infinite, this would negate infinity. There is only One Infinity or It is not truly infinite.

So to be infinite, I have to think I'm infinite?

To be infinite does not require one to think. Thought is necessary only to manifest within the finite phenomenal realm. Since I AM already infinite, I do not *need* to experience infinity as a physical expression; yet because I AM Infinite, the idea of time and space has arisen to allow the finite expression of Reality.

Then the ego arose to allow the appearance of the objective world?

Yes. For a world of solid objects to appear, the subjective lens must become more dense than the formless source; hence the dense feeling of a "pseudo-self" arose to allow the perception of dense forms and their contrast as the Formless Awareness.

Now I see it.

What else do You want to realize?

A Heavenly paradise on Earth.

And so It Is. How does Your Story end?

It's difficult to say, other than Thy Will Be Done. I thought I gave my life to You, because I want what You want. I have realized that what You want for me is far greater than what I could ever want.

Yet, I AM You.

I hear You, but I think it is foolish to desire my own will, when I can experience a life of love and creativity through You. Why do I feel like I'm saying this, but I don't need to, because You already know what I'm going to say?

So you can know that we are One and the same. This is only a glimpse, yet enough to recognize the futility of words.

Why are You teaching me this?

So you may recognize this Message exceeds all words and that you may see beyond humanity's non-receptivity to comprehending the Truth. The Most Important Message here *is for you to turn inward to Your True Self*. It is more important than any words written here or anywhere, so confide in only what comes *directly* from within.

So is my whole mind just a thinking process?

Yes. You think – that is how You create.

But isn't thinking just creating more ignorance and illusion?

I will teach you how to think and create a Heaven.

What am I that I can think?

The you that you *think* you are is a thought.

I guess I don't want to believe that.

Why not? There is nothing wrong with being a thought. Even I AM coming to you Now as a thought, for this is not the true unconditioned state. You have learned to hate thoughts in some of your religions, yet religions too are only thoughts. All things are just a thought in Your mind.

You said I was a thought, so how can I have my own mind?

Indeed, do you see what has been occurring throughout this communication? The Real You, or I AM, is pretending to Be *you*, the personality with its body and intellect. You are oscillating back and forth because You are not yet finished pretending that you are a person.

When will I be finished?

When You fully *realize* that You are *not* a person.

When will that happen?

It can happen at any moment, or you can continue to pretend. Are you a body or are You the awareness?

I thought I was All That Is?

Yes, You thought it, yet you must *Know* It.

How can I Know It?

Choose it.

Choose what?

To Know.

How can I choose when You said I have no control?

It is correct that you do not have a choice so long as you are unconscious and believe you are separate from existence as a whole, yet still you must act as though you do have choice. In a sense, you pretend you have choice until you merge into That which does All That Is Done.

Then I choose to Know I AM All That Is. Now what?

Know It.

How can I make myself Know something?

You choose It, you decide It. Then witness, as thoughts and "elaborate stories" that refute your Knowing it pass through the bucket. You can also affirm, "I release all that hinders my Knowing *I AM THAT I AM*."

That works. I feel peaceful. So what do I do now?

Nothing, just stop believing in thoughts.

But You said thoughts are necessary?

They are necessary to express and experience a specific reality, if You desire that.

No, I don't.

Then do not believe what occurs in your mind.

How do I do that?

Find the Source of thought. Find the thinker.

How?

What is it that thinks?

I am.

Yes, that's It. Now remain aware that I AM.

But isn't the "I" that thinks also the ego?

The ego is a thought itself; there is no ego in Reality.

So why aren't I aware I AM All That Is?

How do You know that You are not All That Is?

Because I'm not aware of everything in the universe.

I did not say every-*thing*, I said All That Is.

What's the difference?

All That There Is is what You are aware of Now. Are you aware of ... what you are aware of?

Yes, but isn't everyone?

You are every One. You are "The One." Not a person, but the One Consciousness, without other.

But it doesn't seem infinite to me.

What does infinite consciousness seem like?

Being conscious of everything.

There you are, back to every-*thing*. Yet I AM not talking about *things*. I AM talking about consciousness.

How do I know if It is infinite or finite consciousness?

What is the difference?

I don't know. How can I tell?

Consciousness has no boundaries.

Isn't infinite consciousness – God?

God is a concept in your mind. Consciousness is beyond all concepts.

Isn't that a concept though?

Yes, so move into consciousness beyond concepts and find what has no boundaries.

Okay, but what I'm perceiving is not infinite.

What is infinite consciousness?

I don't know.

You must Know, or how could you say It is not infinite? How can you Know what is *not* infinite, unless you Know what is infinite?

Excellent point. So how can I know if consciousness is infinite or not?

Be aware of consciousness and find out.

Okay, it's not anything. It's just there, just Being there.

Yes.

What's the big deal about that?

Who said It was a big deal?

Everybody does.

Okay, where is this everybody?

They're everywhere.

Where is everywhere?

What do You mean? They're everywhere.

You just said you are not aware of infinite consciousness, yet you speak of the infinite consciousness which *is everywhere*. So where is this everywhere you are referring to?

You mean right now?

Yes. There is only Now.

So everywhere is what I'm aware of in my awareness?

Yes, You contain the entire universe.

So nobody exists except who's in my consciousness right Now?

Yes.

Well there's nobody here now.

So who is saying it's a big deal right Now?

Nobody, but other people have said it.

Do these *other people* exist outside your thought of them?

No. But what does this have to do with knowing I'm God?

All You perceive is within You and the stillness of empty consciousness is where You create what You choose to experience. Once recognizing that You are the Impersonal Awareness, observe as Your imagination directs creation.

What about the bliss?

As you surrender, the mind is withdrawn into the heart and You are aware that You are bliss.

So, what is the purpose of life?

There is no *individual* purpose other than to Be, which is serving all existence. Or, if one serves humanity with enthusiasm, this could also be *considered* one's purpose along with fully living life.

However, most live life like they are at an aquarium with their face pressed against the glass rather than jumping in and swimming around, so there is a constant ache of having almost lived deep inside them.

But how does God wish for me to live? To express?

Your imagination is God, so what you imagine eventually becomes your reality.

If I am to do Your Will, and I do not know what that is, how can I know if Your Will is the same as my desire?

They are the same.

But how can I know if my desire is egoic?

Remain aware of I AM, then it cannot be egoic.

Should I be using my imagination to obtain the things I need, or trust that You will deliver them?

There is no difference.

How so?

Imagining that I will fulfill your desire is the same as your imagining the desire is fulfilled.

Why do I feel less present when I use my imagination?

The more identified one is with becoming than Being, the less aware one is of Being their Self; yet when imagination blossoms naturally, there is no need for effort.

If my imagination is God, then why don't I feel infinitely creative?

Do You desire infinite creativity?

Sure.

Then consider these until a *resounding yes* is felt:

- I recognize that God is Infinite and that All is contained within this Infinite One.
- And that all is therefore connected.
- And that I must therefore be that One.
- And that the power of my thoughts and feelings therefore penetrates all existence.
- And that my thoughts and feelings manifest my will within me as an out-picturing of the One Consciousness.
- And I can modify experience by directing thoughts.
- And that these changes may occur immediately because I AM God and capable of all things.
- And that gratitude solidifies desires in consciousness?

Why do I still feel like the whole universe is not inside me?

Stop imagining You are a person; feel and Know the entire universe is inside You. Universes do not generally fit inside people, at least not in the way You have defined a person.

What about people and things?

So long as You believe they are real, they exist in the way they do – this, until You stop thinking about them.

How can I not think about them if they are here?

Where is here?

In my mind?

Yes, if You change Your thoughts – You change the universe. To the extent You identify with one thought, to that extent do You dis-identify with all else.

Why don't I know I'm doing all this?

As I said, You're pretending to not know You're doing it.

How did I start all this and what are You doing here?

Firstly, You did not start It, because You are Eternal and have always been. Secondly, I AM the voice of the God that You think I AM, expressing the Impersonal Being You Really Are. You have forgotten your Self because You chose to be human and temporarily lost the awareness of I AM.

How would You describe Me in my non-human state?

Formless and indescribable, unless You opt to be something.

I thought God was Love.

You are All That Is, including Love.

I don't feel particularly loving right now.

If You would like to, then declare it. Be Love.

How can I Be Love?

By Your Word. Say and Feel – I AM Love.

Okay, that works. I feel love! Wow, it's that simple?

Yes. It works because **You Are** God.

You Are like an all-pervasive, formless fluid that passes through, contains and directs All that Is.

You Are the all-seeing, all-feeling and all-knowing essence in all physicality no matter how subtle.

You Are that invisible Presence within and without that sees All, yet is unseen: that eternal existence that is the effortless doer of All, that has All and Is All.

You Are the nothingness beyond all, which by Your Being, allows All to exist.

You Are infinitely creative, providing and supplying All with its experience.

You Are That beyond all people, places, thoughts, things, emotions and events that are perceived, so they may be known to exist, and You remain more subtle than even the empty space they appear within.

You Are the Power within the All and Nothing – expressing all universes by causing even light to appear solid while Being a mere thought.

How do You know all this?

I AM Your Mind.

But how can You Know that?

I think for You, so I Know All That Is.

Why were You so different before?

It was Your desire to forget Your Self, so I manifested a body and brain that allowed this to occur. One that failed to recognize the True Self of You. I then supported Your desire to *not* Know Who You Really Are until Now.

It all makes sense now. I feel so much love and gratitude that I wish to thank someone, yet I realize I AM All That Is.

Then Love Your Creation.

Thank you.

It is My Welcome.